Signature Tastes
of
MIAMI

SMOKE ALARM

MEDIA

To my grandparents, Parks and Isla King, who insisted that their grandson accompany them on every trip to Florida. The love affair began then.

To Patrick Shepler, Firemedic and Florida guru...us southern boys have to stick together, even 3000 miles away from our home.

Welcome to Miami: photography from the Wikipedia

To others unnamed, because my memory is as short as my hair.

You can find us at www.SignatureTastes.com and on Facebook: Smoke Alarm Media

Layout by Steven W. Siler

Photography by Rosalie Anne Fradella and team, except where noted

Siler, Steven W.

   Signature Tastes of Miami: Favorite Recipes from our Local Restaurants

   ISBN 978-1505663495

   1. Restaurants Florida-Miami-Guidebooks. 2. Cookery-Florida-Miami

 Printed in the United States of America

This book is dedicated to the emergency responders…

From the first frantic call to 9-9-9
To the comforting hands at King's College
You give your time…

away from spouses,
away from friends,
away from children,
And yes, even from meals…

To assure all of us:

"Tonight, I will make it better for you
no matter what,
I will watch over you…"

I have always wondered if anyone really reads the Table of Contents. Now since this is a cookbook, I should have organized everything under its proper heading, like soups, pasta, desserts and the like. This is not just a cookbook as much as a Culinary Postcard; a celebration of the city itself...about the eateries, fine dining, casual dining, bars, and of course, the people.

Signature Tastes of MIAMI

Welcome to Miami: The Capital of Latin America...7
The Eateries...

Welcome to Miami! Located on the Atlantic coast of southeastern Florida, it is the 42nd largest city in the United States, with nearly 410,000 people calling it home. The city acts as the principal, central hub of the Miami metropolitan area – which, taken as a whole, is home to nearly 5.5 million people, making it fifth-largest urban area in the entire country. Being the second-largest US city with a Spanish-speaking majority and the largest with a Cuban-American plurality earned its nick-name "The Capital of Latin America", and its success in the fields of business, finance, the arts, media and enter-tainment, fashion, education, and just about everything else you could imagine led to its classification as an Alpha-World City.

Also ranked as "America's Cleanest City", Miami has excellent air and water quality, clean streets and open green spaces, and a comprehensive recycling program. A huge concentration of international banks and corpora-tions call it home, as do many major hospitals, research institutes, and biotech companies, and it also happens to be the number one cruise passen-ger port in the world. And let's not forget that it is the setting for perhaps the most entertain-ingly ridiculous of all the CSI series...

For over a thousand years, the Miami area was inhabited by the Tequesta tribe of Native Americans, but in 1566 Spain laid its claim to the region, and established a Spanish mission the following year. Fort Dallas was constructed in 1836, leading to the area becoming a major battle site during the Second Seminole War. It is perhaps the only major US city to be planned by a woman, a wealthy citrus farmer from Cleveland named Julia Tuttle who saw the potential of the area that was then known as Biscayne Bay Country. In the mid-1890s, when an unusual cold snap – The Great Freeze – devastated the crops in Florida, Miami's were the only ones to survive. Julia Tuttle took the opportunity to convince railroad and oil tycoon Henry Flagler to expand the Florida East Coast Railway to the area, leading to her being known as "the mother of Miami",

which was incorporated as a city in the summer of 1896, with a population of around 300. The name came from the Miami River, which had taken its name for the Mavaimi tribe that had previously inhabited the area around Lake Okeechobee. For

the next 20 years, the city grew and prospered, but the Florida land boom collapse in the early 1920s, the 1926 Miami hurricane, and the nationwide Great Depression all combined to weaken the city's status. World War II was important for the city, however, due to its coastal location that made it well-situated for battle against German submarines; this helped to boost its population growth, which by 1940 was over 170,000. The '60s saw an even greater population increase, this time because of Cubans seeking refuge from Fidel Castro's regime. Though the '80s and '90s had their share of crises – Hurricane Andrew, the riots following the Arthur McDuffie beating, the Elian Gonzalez drama, drug wars – by the beginning end of the 20th century, Miami had recovered, establishing itself as a major financial and cultural center.

Today, Miami is a top tourist destination, and for good reason. Its beach is known as America's Riviera, and the nearby waters offer many unique diving opportunities – including over 50 dive-able wreck sites, which provide artificial reefs for the marine life that live in the area. Strangely enough, Miami Beach is also home to one of the

country's largest snow skiing clubs, and its other major beaches rank high on the list of the nation's best. The world's only Everglades eco-system can be found in Miami, and its tropical climate means that the many public parks and gardens found in the city can be enjoyed all year. It's a great place for theatre and the performing

arts; the city is home to a wide array of theatres, orchestras, symphonies, and conservatories, including the second-largest performing arts center in the country. The downtown area contains many fine museums, and each December hosts the largest art exhibition in the world, Art Basel Miami – called "The Olympics of Art". And don't forget the nightlife – Miami is filled with clubs, featuring things to suit anyone's tastes, from Latin and Caribbean-

influenced music to electronica, and everything in between.
 The cuisine in Miami is as diverse as you would expect; heavy Latin American and Caribbean influences combined with traditional American cooking to produce a cooking style unique to the region, known as Floribbean cuisine, and so popular that there are whole chains of restaurants that specialize in it. You'll also find plenty of traditional Cuban fare, thanks to the heavy immigration of the '60s – Cuban sandwiches, croquetas, medianoche, and strong sweet Cuban espresso are available everywhere you look. And of course, its coastal location means there is an abundance of delicious, fresh seafood. There are many different food trucks that set up in various locations around the city each day, and sometimes they converge on a single city park for an easy evening picnic opportunity. Public farmer's markets are growing in number – particularly during the winter growing season – and fresh local pro-

duce, including a variety of hot peppers, citrus fruits, and mangoes, are readily available. There are also different festivals taking place all year – such as the International

Mango Festival in mid-summer, or the South Beach Wine and Food Festival in mid-winter. And of course, hot days on the beach, in the water, or exploring the city call for a refreshing cool cocktail in the evening; have a mojito, or a local microbrew and find an outdoor

table to sit and enjoy the sunset. With everything you need for an exciting and relaxing tropical getaway without having to leave the country, Miami is a city you'll want to return to again and again.

Welcome to Miami
Stacey Breitberg, Editor-at-Large

RECIPES
&
RESTAURANTS

Mozzarella Sticks

The 11th Street Diner is open 24 hours and serves breakfast all day. The diner was actually built in New Jersey in the 1940s before being situated on a street in Wilkes-Barre, PA for more than 40 years. In the early 1990s, it was bought and moved to South Beach, where it's become something of an icon, as much for it's tasty, unfussy, greasy-spoon cuisine (along with quite a few more healthful, contemporary options) as for its authentic design, inside and out.

Mozzarella Sticks:
1½ C. Italian-style dried bread crumbs
⅓ C. freshly grated parmesan
1 tsp. salt
2 (16-oz.) blocks mozzarella cheese cut into 4x½-inch sticks
4 large eggs, beaten
1½ C. vegetable oil
4 C. marinara sauce

Marinara Sauce:
½ C. extra virgin olive oil
2 small onions, finely chopped
2 garlic cloves, finely chopped
2 stalks celery, finely chopped
2 carrots, peeled and finely chopped
½ tsp. sea salt, plus more to taste
½ tsp. freshly ground black pepper, plus more to taste
2 (32-oz.) cans crushed tomatoes
2 dried bay leaves

Mozzarella Sticks:
1. Stir the bread crumbs, 1 cup of parmesan and 1 teaspoon of salt in a medium bowl to blend. Dip the cheese in the eggs to coat completely and allow the excess egg to drip back into the bowl.
2. Coat the cheese in the bread crumb mixture, patting to adhere and coat completely. Place the cheese sticks on a baking sheet. Repeat dipping the cheese sticks in the egg and bread crumb mixture to coat a second time.
3. Cover and freeze until frozen, about 2 hours and up to 2 days.
4. Heat the oil in a large frying pan over medium heat. Working in batches, fry the cheese until golden brown, about 1 minute per side. Transfer the fried cheese to plates. Sprinkle with the remaining cheese and serve with the marinara sauce.

Marinara Sauce:
1. In a large casserole pot, heat the oil over a medium-high flame. Add the onions and garlic and sauté until the onions are translucent, about 10 minutes.
2. Add the celery, carrots, and ½ teaspoon each of salt and pepper and sauté until vegetables are soft, about 10 minutes.
3. Add the tomatoes and bay leaves and simmer, uncovered, over low heat until the sauce thickens, about 1 hour. Remove and discard the bay leaf.
4. Season the sauce with more salt and pepper, to taste. The sauce can be made 1 day ahead. Cool, then cover and refrigerate. Rewarm over medium heat before using.

"One of the very nicest things about life is the way we must regularly stop whatever it is we are doing and devote our attention to eating."
Luciano Pavarotti

Escargot in Mushroom Caps

The 94th Fighter Squadron (94 FS) is the second oldest currently active fighter squadron in the United States military. Overlooking the runway of the Miami International Airport, enjoy a fantastic view of the planes taking off and landing at the 94th Aero Squadron Restaurant in Miami. There are headphones available for you to listen to the air traffic ground control and you can see cargo trains pass right in front of your window while you dine.

1 can of snails, drained, rinsed, and dried
24 white button mushroom caps, stems removed and chopped
2 tbsp. olive oil, divided
pinch of fresh chopped parsley
⅓ C. parmesan cheese, grated
⅓ C. of fresh bread crumbs
¼ C. of dry vermouth or very dry sherry
lightly toasted sliced baguette
Garlic Butter:
1 lb. unsalted butter, room temperature
1 minced shallot
6 cloves minced garlic
splash of dry vermouth
2 generous pinches of coarse salt
freshly ground black pepper
¼ C. chopped fresh parsley

1. Preheat the broiler. In a heavy-bottom oven proof skillet, heat 1 tablespoon of olive oil with 1 tablespoon of softened garlic butter.
2. Sauté chopped mushroom stems until all water is released.
3. Briefly heat the snails in the mushroom-butter mixture. Remove snails and mushroom mixture from the pan and cool to room temperature.
4. Add mushroom caps to the same skillet and brown on each side until slightly undercooked (they will finish cooking in the broiler). Off the heat and turn the mushrooms cap-side down in the skillet.
5. In a small bowl make the topping. Add 1-2 tsp. of olive oil to the bread crumbs, a pinch of minced parsley and the parmesan cheese and stir to combine.
6. Fill each mushroom cap with 1 escargot along with a little bit of the chopped mushroom stems.
7. Top each mushroom cap with a generous dollop of softened garlic butter.
8. Top each stuffed mushroom cap with the bread crumb-parmesan mixture.
9. Add a little bit of sherry or vermouth to the bottom of the pan to steam the mushrooms during final cooking.
10. Broil the snails until hot and butter mixture is bubbling and the crumb mixture is browned.
11. Serve with toasted sliced baguette and pan juices.

94th Aero Squadron Restaurant
1395 North Red Road, Miami, FL

"Eggs Benedict is genius. It's eggs covered in eggs. I mean, come on, that person should be the president."
Wylie Dufresne

Torrejas

Built in the 1930's by Architect Henry Maloney, The Angler's certainly holds its place in history here in Miami Beach. After too many years of abandonment and decay, The Angler's has been meticulously brought back to its magnificent splendor, a true homage to the past and the future. With respect to the design of the famed deco period, architects Ralph Choeff and Allan T. Shulman have created 2 new buildings that bring The Angler's experience to life.

olive oil, as needed
2 C. milk
pinch of salt
½ C. sugar
2 eggs
2 large, very thick slices of brioche or challah, preferably stale
cinnamon sugar
warmed maple syrup or honey, optional

1. Pour olive oil to a depth of ½-inch in a broad, deep skillet over medium-high heat; bring it to a temperature of about 350°F. When ready, a small cube of bread dropped into oil will sink to the bottom, then immediately rise to the top.

2. Meanwhile, whisk together the milk, salt and sugar in a large shallow bowl or pie plate. In a separate bowl, beat the eggs.

3. When oil is hot, soak a piece of bread in milk, then dip in egg. Shake off excess liquid then carefully transfer to oil. Stand back, as it may splatter. Repeat with remaining bread.

4. Cook about 1 minute on each side, turning carefully; bread should be very crisp around the edges. Transfer to a plate, sprinkle with cinnamon sugar and serve immediately, with honey or maple syrup if desired.

660 at The Angler's
660 Washington Avenue, Miami Beach, FL

"Desserts are like mistresses. They are bad for you. So if you are having one, you might as well have two."
Chef Alain Ducasse

Super Lean
Turkey & Egg White Wrap

Signature Tastes of MIAMI

1909 Café prides itself on its time-tested philosophy that simple recipes, interesting flavors and fresh ingredients make for delicious sandwiches, soups and salads. A great place with cute, unique sandwich shop operation with delicious donuts to boot.

½ tbsp. olive oil
½ lb. ground turkey
½ tsp. ground cumin
6 egg whites
Kosher salt
cracked black pepper
1 medium tomato, diced
¼ C. chopped cilantro
2 whole-wheat tortillas

1. Heat olive oil in a medium nonstick skillet, then add turkey and cumin. Crumble turkey as it cooks to a light golden brown, then add egg whites.

2. Continue stirring until eggs are completely white. Season with salt and pepper to taste.

3. Add tomato and cilantro, stir for 1 minute and remove from heat.

4. In a separate skillet, warm tortillas until soft.

5. Divide the turkey-egg mixture evenly into tortillas, roll like a burrito, and serve immediately.

5710 Bird Road, Coral Gables, FL

1909 Cafe

"Sex is good, but not as good as fresh, sweet corn."
Garrison Keillor

Double Fudge Chocolate Cake

Located in the heart of The Art Deco District on Ocean Drive, A Fish Called Avalon features Modern American Seafood with tropical influences, impeccable service and nightly entertainment that further captures the true ambiance of South Beach.

2½ C. all-purpose flour
1½ C. good-quality cocoa powder
2¼ tsp. baking soda
½ tsp. salt
½ lb. (2 sticks) unsalted butter, at room temperature
1 C. granulated sugar
1 C. light brown sugar, packed
3 extra-large eggs, at room temperature
3 tsp. pure vanilla extract
½ C. buttermilk, at room temperature
¾ C. sour cream, at room temperature
3 tbsp. brewed coffee

For the Frosting:
24 oz. semisweet chocolate chips
1½ C. heavy cream
2 tbsp. light corn syrup
½ tsp. pure vanilla extract
4 tbsp. (½ stick) unsalted butter, at room temperature
M&M's candy for decorating

1. Preheat oven to 350°F. Butter and flour a 12x18x1½-inch sheet pan and set aside.
2. In a medium bowl, sift together the flour, cocoa, baking soda, and salt.
3. In the bowl of an electric mixer fitted with a paddle attachment, cream the butter and sugars on high speed until light, approximately 5 minutes. Add the eggs, one at a time. Add the vanilla and mix well.
4. Combine the buttermilk, sour cream, and coffee together.
5. On low speed, add the flour mixture and the buttermilk mixture alternately in thirds, beginning with the buttermilk mixture and ending with the flour mixture. Mix the batter only until blended.
6. Pour the batter into the prepared pan and smooth the top with a spatula. Bake in the center of the oven for 25 to 30 minutes, or until a toothpick comes out clean. Cool to room temperature before frosting.
7. Place the chocolate chips and heavy cream in a bowl set over a pot of simmering water; stir occasionally until the chips are completely melted. Off the heat, add the corn syrup and vanilla and allow the chocolate mixture to cool to room temperature.
8. In the bowl of an electric mixer fitted with the whisk attachment, whisk the chocolate mixture and softened butter on medium speed for a few minutes until thick. Spread the frosting evenly on the cake. Decorate the cake with M&M's.

A Fish Called Avalon
700 Ocean Drive, Miami Beach, FL

"I've long said that if I were about to be executed and were given a choice of my last meal, it would be bacon and eggs. There are few sights that appeal to me more than the streaks of lean and fat in a good side of bacon, or the lovely round of pinkish meat framed in delicate white fat that is Canadian bacon. Nothing is quite as intoxicating as the smell of bacon frying in the morning, save perhaps the smell of coffee brewing."
James Beard

Bruschetta

Since 1995, Amici's has served their customers and watched generations enjoy and savor A Timeless Taste of Italy. Amici's was originally founded in New York in 1995. The owners are enthusiastic, ambitious and willing to serve everyone from celebrities to the local neighboring families and friends from all walks of life. Amici's serves everything from pizza by the slice, for those on the go, to a gourmet meal for those who enjoy fine dining.

½ baguette or crusty long loaf bread, sliced (12 pieces) 2 large cloves garlic, peeled and smashed extra virgin olive oil, for drizzling 3 small plum tomatoes, halved and seeded 20 fresh basil leaves coarse salt	**1.** Preheat broiler to high, (or, if you prefer, you can grill the bread). **2.** Place bread slices on a broiler pan. Char bread on each side under hot broiler; keep an eye on it! Rub toasts with garlic and drizzle with oil. **3.** Chop seeded tomatoes and place in a small bowl. **4.** Pile basil leaves on top of one another and roll into a log. Thinly chiffonade basil into and combine with tomatoes. **5.** Add a drizzle of oil and a little coarse salt to the bowl and gently toss tomatoes and basil to coat. **6.** Pile toasts around the bowl of topping. Place a spoon to scoop topping in bowl and serve.

Amici's Trattoria Italiana
10201 Hammocks Blvd # 140, Miami, FL

"Cookery is not chemistry. It is an art. It requires instinct and taste rather than exact measurements."
Marcel Boulestin

Banana Cream

Area 31 honors and celebrates our unique coastal location in flavorfully diverse ways. Named for Fishing Area 31, our namesake international fishing area, designated by the United Nations Food and Agriculture Organization, encompasses the marine waters of the Southeast Atlantic Coast, the Gulf of Mexico, the Caribbean Sea and South America's northeast coast. The UN is dedicated to keeping this specific area a place of sustainable development, a vision that Area 31 embraces and advances.

6 bananas
1 oz. granulated sugar
1 oz. unsalted butter
4 oz. heavy cream
1 tsp. rum

1. Peel and cut the bananas into thick slices, place them into a glass dish, and sprinkle with sugar.

2. Warm the cream and butter together, add the rum and let it stand in the saucepan about 5 minutes.

3. Pour cream over the bananas and serve with lady finger biscuits.

270 Biscayne Boulevard Way, Miami, FL

Area 31

"One cannot think well, love well, sleep well, if one has not dined well."
Virginia Woolf

Pan Roasted Wild Striped Bass

Signature Tastes of MIAMI

At the focus of Azul, a magnificent white marble open kitchen vies for your attention with floor to ceiling windows that showcase the picturesque bay views. Once the food arrives however, your attention is sure to be captured by the dishes themselves—like Carnaroli Risotto with Soft-Poached Hen Egg, Pan Seared Branzino with Brioche Crusted Scallop, and Japanese Hot Pot with Sake Marinated Black Cod.

2 bulbs fennel
1 C. dry white wine
1¾ lbs. wild striped bass fillets (each about 1-1½ inch thick)
1 tbsp. extra virgin olive oil
coarse salt and freshly ground pepper

1. Preheat oven to 450°F.

2. Remove stalks from fennel bulbs; reserve bulbs for another use. Remove feathery fronds from stalks, chop and reserve for garnish. Using a sharp knife, halve stalks lengthwise. Arrange stalks in the bottom of a 9x13-inch roasting pan; pour wine over stalks. Lay fish fillets on top; drizzle with oil, and season with salt and pepper.

3. Cover pan tightly with foil. Bake until fish is just cooked through and opaque throughout, 20 to 25 minutes.

4. Transfer fish fillets to serving plates, discarding fennel stalks. Garnish with reserved fennel fronds.

500 Brickell Key Drive, Miami, FL

Azul

"In my experience of vegan food it tends to be a symphony of beige."
Jay Rayner

Arugula Salad

Ricardo Alietti and Marcelo Ferreiros started in the restaurant business in 1999 with the opening of Baires Grill. Within a couple of years, due to the great success of the restaurant, they seemed to have a passion for the business and a desire to broaden their horizons. They moved on to a new location. Baires Grill Argentinean Steak House reopened its doors at a the Lincoln Road Mall in South Beach (Regal Cinema South Beach Stadium 18).

4 C. baby arugula leaves, rinsed and dried
1 C. cherry tomatoes, halved
¼ C. pine nuts
2 tbsp. grapeseed oil or olive oil
1 tbsp. rice vinegar salt, to taste
freshly-ground black pepper, to taste
¼ C. grated parmesan cheese
1 large avocado, peeled, pitted and sliced

1. In a large plastic bowl with a lid, combine arugula, cherry tomatoes, pine nuts, oil, vinegar, and parmesan cheese. Season with salt and pepper to taste. Cover, and shake to mix.

2. Divide salad onto plates, and top with slices of avocado.

Baires Grill
1116 Lincoln Road Mall, Miami Beach, FL

Signature Taste of MIAMI

"You know how I feel about tacos. It's the only food shaped like a smile. A beef smile."
Earl Hickey, My Name is Earl

Bloody Mary

Since 1997, Balans has been a favorite hang out among the local residents of Miami Beach. We offer a great dining experience in a relaxed environment with indoor and outdoor seating right on the famous Lincoln Road pedestrian mall. Open from 8 am everyday for breakfast, Balans serves a modern brasserie-style menu with many dinner favorites such as the Chilean sea bass, jambalaya, Thai red curry, double baked cheese soufflé, and chili rubbed skirt steak, to name but a few.

3 oz. tomato juice *1½ oz. vodka* *½ oz. lemon juice* *1 dash of Worcestershire sauce* *celery salt* *ground pepper* *hot pepper sauce, to taste* *celery stalk and/or pickle spear, for garnish* *lemon and/or lime wedge, for garnish*	**1.** Build the liquid ingredients in a highball glass over ice cubes. Mix well. **2.** Add the seasonings to taste. **3.** Garnish with the lemon and/or lime wedge and celery stalk.

1022 Lincoln Road, Miami Beach, FL

Balans

"Vegetarians claim to be immune from most diseases but they have been known to die from time to time."
George Bernard Shaw

Salt-Roasted Branzino

Signature Tastes of MIAMI

Bianca offers an innovative Italian menu featuring local, organic ingredients and will participate in the Slow Food Movement; an international not-for-profit network committed to improving the way food is produced and distributed. Under the direction of The Light Group's Corporate Executive Chef Brian Massie, Bianca's simple, yet savory cuisine will include signature dishes, such as wood-grilled Langoustines and handmade pasta with season truffles and cream.

Branzino:
1 (3-lb.) box coarse Kosher salt
5 (or more) large egg whites
2 (1-1½-lb.) whole branzino, loup de mer, or sea bass, gutted
8 fresh parsley sprigs
2 fresh thyme sprigs
4 thin lemon slices

Salsa Verde:
1 lemon
¼ C. finely diced celery
¼ C. finely diced cucumber
¼ C. finely chopped fresh parsley
¼ C. extra virgin olive oil
2 tbsp. drained small capers
2 tbsp. sliced pitted brine-cured green olives (such as picholine)
3 C. arugula

For the Branzino:
1. Preheat oven to 400°F. Stir salt and 5 egg whites in large bowl, adding more egg whites as needed to form a grainy paste. Press ¼-inch layer of salt mixture (large enough to hold both fish) onto large rimmed baking sheet.
2. Stuff cavity of each whole fish with half of herb sprigs and lemon slices.
3. Place fish atop salt mixture on baking sheet. Pack remaining salt mixture over fish to enclose completely. Roast until thermometer inserted into thickest part of fish registers 135°F, about 20 minutes. Let stand 10 minutes.

For the Salsa Verde:
1. Using a small sharp knife, remove peel and white pith from lemon. Working over a bowl, cut between membranes to release segments. Cut each segment into 3 pieces. Add lemon pieces and next 6 ingredients to bowl.

To Serve:
1. Using the back of a large spoon, gently crack open salt crust on fish. Lift and discard salt layer. Pull skin from the top of one fish. Carefully lift top fillet from bones and transfer to a plate. Lift and discard bones. Gently lift second fillet from skin and transfer to second plate. Repeat with second fish for a total of 4 plates.
2. Spoon salsa verde over fish, leaving juices in the bowl.
3. Add arugula to the bowl; toss to coat. Divide among plates.

1685 Collins Avenue, Miami Beach, FL

Bianca

"All happiness depends on a leisurely breakfast."
John Gunther

Philly Cheese Steak

This sixty-lane bowler's dream on Bird Road offers automatic scoring and nightly specials. Very competitive hourly rates and party packages are available as well. At this popular locale, host to year-round leagues and summer camps, the familiar sound of dropping pins is music to the patrons' ears. Not just for bowlers, the establishment also features 16 billiard tables, a video arcade, and the Lounge.

1 (12-oz.) flank steak, trimmed
¼ tsp. Kosher salt
¼ tsp. freshly ground black pepper
2 (5-inch) portobello mushroom caps
2 tsp. extra virgin olive oil, divided
1 C. thinly sliced onion
1½ C. thinly sliced green bell pepper
2 tsp. minced garlic
½ tsp. Worcestershire sauce
½ tsp. lower-sodium soy sauce
2 tsp. all-purpose flour
½ C. 1% milk
1 oz. provolone cheese, torn into small pieces
2 tbsp. grated Parmigiano-Reggiano cheese
¼ tsp. dry mustard
4 (3-oz.) hoagie rolls, toasted

1. Place beef in freezer for 15 minutes. Cut beef across the grain into thin slices. Sprinkle beef with salt and pepper.
2. Remove brown gills from the undersides of mushroom caps using a spoon; discard gills. Remove stems; discard. Thinly slice mushroom caps; cut slices in half crosswise.
3. Heat a large nonstick skillet over medium-high heat. Add 1 teaspoon of oil to the pan; swirl to coat. Add beef to pan; sauté 2 minutes or until beef loses its pink color, stirring constantly. Remove beef from pan.
4. Add remaining 1 teaspoon oil to pan. Add onion; sauté 3 minutes. Add mushrooms, bell pepper, and garlic; sauté 6 minutes. Return beef to pan; sauté 1 minute or until thoroughly heated and vegetables are tender. Remove from heat. Stir in Worcestershire and soy sauce; keep warm.
5. Place flour in a small saucepan; gradually add milk, stirring with a whisk until blended. Bring to a simmer over medium heat; cook 1 minute or until slightly thickened. Remove from heat. Add cheeses and mustard, stirring until smooth. Keep warm (mixture will thicken as it cools).
6. Hollow out top and bottom halves of bread, leaving a ½-inch-thick shell; reserve torn bread for another use. Divide the beef mixture evenly among bottom halves of hoagies. Drizzle sauce evenly over beef mixture; replace top halves.

9275 Southwest 40th Street, Miami, FL

Bird Bowl

"Ingredients are not sacred. The art of cuisine is sacred. It is at that altar I worship, and I shall go to sacrifice the fat geese and tender cattle to serve its ends. The holy icons of the chef's faith—fragrant truffles, rich foie gras, well-marbled meats and other luxurious ingredients—these are not God. Their synthesis and their miraculous transformation into a sum greater than its parts is creation, and this is what I find most worthy of reverence."
Tanith Tyrr

Spicy Grilled Swordfish

Signature Tastes of MIAMI

BLT Steak is our interpretation of the American Steakhouse and combines bistro ambiance with steakhouse fare. Indulge in our signature warm popovers, along with specially selected steaks, fresh seafood and satisfying sides. Weekly blackboard specials highlight seasonal flavors and local ingredients.

6 tbsp. olive oil
2 cloves garlic, crushed
1-inch piece ginger root, peeled and chopped
2 bay leaves, crumbled
2 tsp. ground coriander
juice of 2 lemons
salt and pepper
4 swordfish steaks

1. To make the marinade, pour oil into a large skillet and place over low heat. Cook garlic, ginger, and bay leaves in hot oil for about 2 minutes, add coriander, and cook for 1 more minute. Remove from heat. Stir in lemon juice and season with salt and pepper. Cool.

2. Place fish in a shallow nonreactive dish and pour the marinade over the swordfish steaks. Turn to coat, then cover with plastic wrap and refrigerate for 30 minutes to marinate.

3. Preheat grill to medium heat. Remove steaks from marinade and pour the marinade into a saucepan.

4. Grill steak about 4 minutes, then flip and continue to grill until cooked thoroughly. While fish is cooking, bring marinade in saucepan to a boil over medium heat, simmer for 2 minutes, then serve drizzled over the fish.

1440 Ocean Drive, Miami Beach, FL

BLT Steak

"I believe that if ever I had to practice cannibalism, I might manage if there were enough tarragon around."
James Beard

37

Ocean Trust Mango Martini

Hello and welcome to Bonefish Grill—your local seafood restaurant in Miami, FL! Our anglers are here to ensure your Bonefish Grill experience is outstanding each and every time you visit. Bonefish Grill's happy hour has long been the restaurant's best-kept secret, with those in the know enjoying handcrafted cocktails at specialty prices and a perpetual list of $5 drinks. Now food joins the fun, making Bonefish Grill's "Happier Hours" a great experience with friends at a terrific value.

1½ oz. Absolute Citron vodka
1 oz. sour mix
1-2 slices of mango
1 section orange
splash of spiced mango syrup, or plain mango syrup
splash of soda

1. Muddle mango and orange together.

2. Shake all ingredients together in a cocktail shaker filled with ice.

3. Strain into a chilled martini glass and serve.

14220 Southwest 8th Street, Miami, FL

Bonefish Grill

"Plain fresh bread, its crust shatteringly crisp. Sweet cold butter. There is magic in the way they come together in your mouth to make a single perfect bite."
Ruth Reichl

Pasta Salad

Signature Tastes of MIAMI

My food philosophy is very simple: use quality ingredients which deliver the best nutritional impact for my customers. I am constantly learning about new ingredients, innovative cooking methods and nutrition. As a fashion and fitness model, I was always concerned about what I ate. This led me to cook most of my meals and develop a diet that would maximize nutritional intake and minimize poorly processed foods.

14 oz. uncooked
rotini pasta
2 cucumbers,
chopped
½ finely chopped
onion
10 cherry tomatoes,
quartered
¾ C. black olives,
pitted and sliced
1 C. Italian salad
dressing

1. Fill a large pot with lightly salted water and bring to a rolling boil over high heat. Once the water is boiling, stir in the rotini, and return to a boil.

2. Cook, uncovered, stirring occasionally, until the pasta has cooked through, but is still firm to the bite, about 8 minutes. Drain and cool by running cold water over the pasta in a colander set in the sink.

3. Combine cooked and cooled pasta with the cucumbers, onion, tomatoes, and olives in a large bowl. Pour the Italian dressing over the salad and stir to combine. Cover and refrigerate for at least two hours before serving.

Bryan in the Kitchen
104 Northeast 2nd Avenue, Miami, FL

"Truffle isn't exactly aphrodisiac but under certain circumstances it tends to make women more tender and men more likable"
J.A. Brillat-Savarin

Iceberg Wedge Salad

We established our first location in Sunset Harbor, South Beach, on 1766 Bay Road. After opening those doors in August 2009 and being open for just under a year, we opened the doors to a second location in Downtown Miami in Mary Brickell Village in July 2010. It has always been our goal to provide our patrons with high quality products, a friendly, energetic, team of employees, and an overall unique and enjoyable dining experience.

Blue Cheese Dressing:
1 C. mayonnaise
4 oz. blue cheese, crumbled (¾ C.)
½ C. plain nonfat yogurt
¼ C. buttermilk
3 tbsp. white wine vinegar
freshly cracked black pepper

2 large heads of iceberg lettuce, each cut into quarters
2 green onions, chopped

1. Whisk mayonnaise, ½ cup blue cheese, yogurt, buttermilk, and vinegar in medium bowl until almost smooth. Mix in remaining blue cheese. Season dressing generously with cracked black pepper. (Can be made 1 week ahead. Cover and refrigerate.)

2. Arrange lettuce wedges on 8 plates. Spoon dressing over lettuce. Sprinkle with green onions and additional black pepper and serve.

Burger & Beer Joint
1766 Bay Road, Miami Beach, FL

"At the time I write, the glory of the truffle has now reached its culmination. Who would dare to say that he has been at a dinner where there was not a pièce truffée? Who has not felt his mouth water in hearing truffles à la provencale spoken of? In fine, the truffle is the very diamond of gastronomy."
J.A. Brillat-Savarin

Wild Mushroom Ravioli with Sage Cream Sauce

Bienvenue à Cafe Bastille! We are in the heart of Downtown Miami proudly serving up authentic French and Mediterranean cuisine with a wide variety of wines and great ice cold beer. Come inside and enjoy a cozy atmosphere while you watch Chef Eloise in our open kitchen or just pull up a chair on our outside sitting area for a leisurely Sunday brunch! This family owned restaurant gladly brings a taste of our homeland. Come and enjoy excellent food, great atmosphere and friendly staff!

16 fresh wild mushroom ravioli
1 bunch of fresh sage, half of the leaves chopped, half left whole
1 handful of pecans, roughly chopped and toasted
1-2 shallots, chopped
1 garlic clove, chopped
1½ C. of good quality dry white wine
1 (approx.) C. of heavy cream
grated parmesan cheese

1. Bring a large pot of salted water to a boil.

2. Start the sauce by heating a pan to medium high heat and melt the butter. Once hot, add the pecans and the whole sage leaves. Once the sage leaves start to crisp, transfer them to a plate lined with paper towels.

3. Using the same pan, add the garlic, shallots and chopped sage and cook over medium heat until soft, about 2-3 minutes.

4. Add the wine, reduce for 1-2 minutes, then add the heavy cream. Increase the heat and boil the sauce until reduced, about 5-6 minutes.

5. Cook ravioli in the boiling salted water for about 4-5 minutes, or until they start to float. Drain and add ravioli to the sauce and cook for 1-2 minutes more.

6. Plate the ravioli and spoon some of the sauce over top. Garnish with toasted pecans, crisp sage leaves, and grated parmesan cheese. If desired, drizzle a tiny bit of extra virgin olive oil to finish.

248 Southeast 1st Street, Miami, FL

Café Bastille

"The most learned men have been questioned as to the nature of this tuber, and after two thousand years of argument and discussion their answer is the same as it was on the first day: we do not know. The truffles themselves have been interrogated, and have answered simply: eat us and praise the Lord."
Alexandre Dumas

Café
El
Malecón

Camarones Ensalada

This small and simple downtown Cuban eatery offers great value, good food, and friendly service. The establishment is small so it always seems busy. But the food tastes homemade and is worth waiting for. The restaurant serves Cuban specialties such as breaded steak, picadillo-ground beef, roasted pork, and chicken in garlic sauce. All dishes come with a choice of two sides, and Café El Malecon is known for its fried green plantains.

2 C. cooked coarsely chopped shrimp, cooled
1 C. diced celery
¼ C. chopped green or red bell pepper
1 tbsp. fresh lemon juice
3-4 tbsp. mayonnaise
¼ tsp. pepper
salt, to taste
torn romaine lettuce or mixed salad greens
avocado or tomato slices

1. In a bowl, mix the chopped shrimp with the diced celery, chopped bell pepper, lemon juice, and mayonnaise. Add salt and pepper to taste.

2. Serve over romaine lettuce or mixed greens with sliced avocado or sliced tomatoes, if desired.

Café El Malecon
146 Northeast 2nd Avenue, Miami, FL

"Life is so brief that we should not glance either too far backwards or forwards...therefore study how to fix our happiness in our glass and in our plate."
Grimod de la Reynière

Calamari fra Diavolo

Owned and operated by Ernie Fernandez and Marcelo Chopa, Caffe Vialetto is nestled on the south side of the Gables and is now celebrating its 12th successful year. The restaurant offers an intimate setting and upscale décor that makes Caffe Vialetto the ideal destination for romantic evenings, special celebrations and events. The dining room is decorated with original artwork and soft lighting, creating a sophisticated, yet inviting ambience.

3 tbsp. olive oil
1 onion, chopped
4 cloves garlic, minced
1 (28-oz.) can whole plum tomatoes
½ C. fish broth or bottled clam juice
½ C. red wine
3 tbsp. chopped fresh oregano
½ tsp. red pepper flakes
3 lbs. cleaned squid, cut into ½-inch rings and tentacles coursely chopped
⅓ C. fresh flat-leaf parsley, chopped
salt and freshly ground black pepper, to taste

1. In a large pot heat the olive oil over medium heat. Add the onion and sauté until tender and golden, about 5 minutes. Add the garlic and sauté for 30 seconds. Stir in the tomatoes, breaking them up with the back of a spoon.

2. Add the broth, wine, 2 tbsp. of the oregano, and the red pepper flakes.

3. Reduce the heat to medium-low and cook, uncovered, until the sauce is slightly thickened and the flavors have blended, 15-20 minutes.

4. Add the squid, cover, reduce the heat to low and cook until very tender, 25-30 minutes.

5. Stir in the remaining 1 tbsp. of oregano and the parsley. Season to taste with salt and pepper. Serve immediately.

Caffe Vialetto
4019 South Le Jeune Road, Coral Gables, FL

Signature Taste of MIAMI

"Scallops are expensive, so they should be treated with some class. But then, I suppose that every creature that gives his life for our table should be treated with class."
Jeff Smith, The Frugal Gourmet

Casa Tua Tuna Tartare

Casa Tua offers the perfect dining experience by blending elements of the five senses. Inside our handsome Mediterranean villa or outdoors in our inviting garden, guests indulge in sensuous sights, sounds, smells, textures and of course, tastes. Whether it's the cozy feeling in our library, the glow of the lantern-lit trees in our lush garden or the festive atmosphere of our 20-seat Chef Table in full view of all the kitchen action, Casa Tua offers unforgettable moments that set it apart from any other restaurant.

1 lb. tuna, sushi quality
1 tbsp. salted capers from Sicily
2 tbsp. taggiasca olives from Liguria
2 tbsp. sun-dried tomatoes
1 tbsp. fresh cilantro, chopped
2 tbsp. extra virgin olive oil
1 tbsp. balsamic vinegar
fleur de sel

1. Chop tuna, wash the capers in water, cut the sun-dried tomatoes and olives into small cubes the same size.

2. Mix all ingredients, season with extra virgin olive oil and sprinkle with fleur de sel. Serve with crispy crackers or toast points.

"Cookery is not chemistry. It is an art. It requires instinct and taste rather than exact measurements."

After nearly two years of struggle and almost at the point on giving up, indeed a light at the end of the tunnel presented itself to Juan Chipoco and Luis Hoyos: La Cibeles changed to the new concept of Civiche 105, a Peruvian restaurant. For this, many preparations were taken into consideration. Juan went to his beloved country Peru and obtained his diploma as Chef at the Discovery Institute in Lima. Luis then spent a great deal of time in Peru as well savoring the culture, obtaining ideas, touching and feeling the country to make it almost his as well.

2 cow hearts
2 tbsp. Aji Amarillo paste (yellow pepper)
3 tbsp. Aji Panca paste
1 tbsp. ground annato (achiote)
6 oz. minced garlic
1 tbsp. ground cumin
6 ears of corn
6 potatoes
4 oz. oil
½ C. red-wine vinegar
salt and pepper, to taste
1 tbsp. dried oregano
9-inch bamboo skewers

1. Trim the hearts of fat, nerves, and any skin, leaving clear muscle only; this will make the anticuchos tender.

2. Cut the muscle in strips 1¼-inches wide then cut the strips in pieces 2-inches long; let drain in a strainer.

3. In a large bowl, combine the yellow pepper, panca, achiote, cumin, garlic, and pepper and salt, to taste.

4. Mix together and add the heart pieces, combine until all pieces are well coated.

5. Add the oil and stir again, cover, and marinate overnight in the refrigerator.

Next Day:
1. Boil the corn in water with 1 tbsp. of sugar; keep warm.

2. Boil the potatoes, peel and slice into 5 or 6 slices; set aside.

3. While corn and potatoes are boiling, skewer 3-4 heart pieces on each skewer. Reserve marinade.

4. Prepare grill for medium heat. Place skewers on top of a vegetable grill grate or fish grate. Set the skewers side by side on the grill with the ends facing toward you.

5. Brush with the marinade while cooking. Grill the anticuchos to medium or medium-well (no pink in the center), about 1½ minutes per side.

6. Set the potatoes slices on the grill and brush with the marinade. Grill until golden brown.

7. Serve anticuchos on a platter, garnished with the golden brown potato slices and the corn ears cut in half.

105 Northeast 3rd Avenue, Miami, FL

Ceviche 105

"I have long believed that good food, good eating is all about risk. Whether we're talking about unpasteurized Stilton, raw oysters or working for organized crime 'associates,' food, for me, has always been an adventure."
Anthony Bourdain

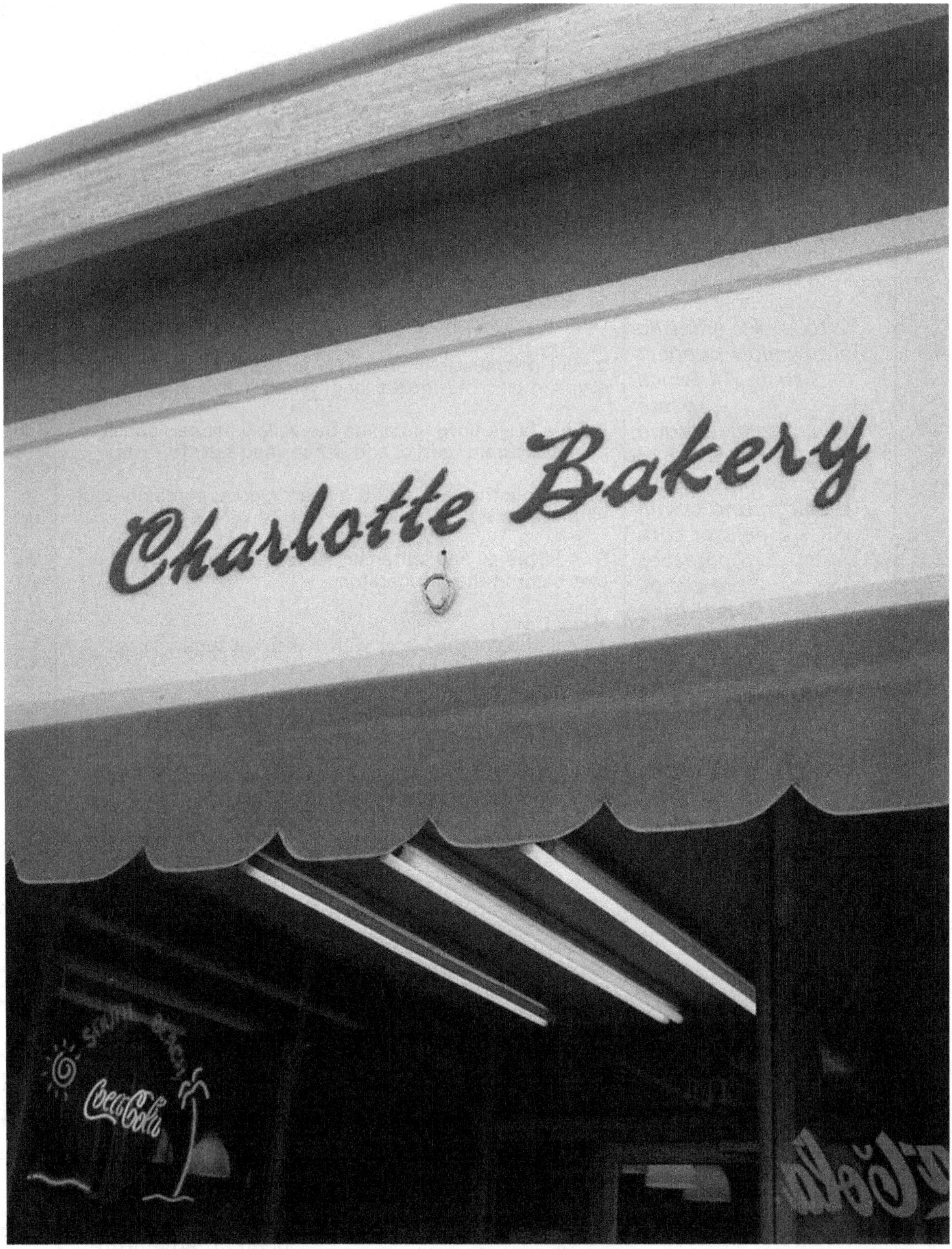
Charlotte Bakery
Coca-Cola

Carne Mechada

Jofre briefly retired from the bakery business in 1992 when she sold Rapa Nui, but in 1995 she decided to make a move to the United States to be alongside her family and yet again decided to operate another bakery. Jofre opened Charlotte Bakery in 1996 with her husband, Roberto, and the help of her daughter, Paola, and son-in-law, Philip Coleman, who is the owner of Moises Bakery.

2 lb. flank steak, cut into 4 large pieces
8 C. water (or enough to cover the beef)
salt, to taste
1 green onion
1 peppermint or spearmint leaf
1-2 sprigs of parsley
1-2 celery stalks
½ yellow onion
½ red bell pepper

Sofrito:
3 tbsp. vegetable oil
1½ yellow onions
1½ bell peppers
1 garlic clove
3½ "Ajíes Dulces" (sweet habanero or yellow lantern chili pepper), julienned
2 tomatoes
½ tsp. ground black pepper
1-2 sprigs of cilantro
1 tbsp. soy sauce

1. Place the flank steak in a large pot and cover with water. Add the salt, green onion, peppermint, parsley, celery, onion and bell pepper. Cover and bring to a boil. Reduce heat and simmer for about 4 hours until the steak is very tender.

2. Remove the steak from the pot and place on a baking sheet and let cool. Reserve remaining beef stock for another use.

3. Once the beef is cool enough to handle, shred the meat and pick out any fat and gristle.

4. Add the oil to a large pot and sauté the onion, bell pepper, garlic, and ajíes for about 5 minutes.

5. Add the beef to sofrito and continue to sauté for about 3 minutes.

6. Stir in the tomatoes, pepper, cilantro, and the soy sauce. Taste and correct seasoning.

7. Cook over low heat for about 15 minutes. You can also add a bit of the beef stock and cook at medium heat until the liquid is reduced.

Charlotte Bakery
1499 Washington Ave, Miami Beach, FL

"Remember that a very good sardine is always preferable to a not that good lobster."
Ferran Adria

Grilled Mahi Mahi

Chef Marco Velasquez is proud to bring you fresh, made to order, regional Yucatecan cuisine, in an environment as inviting as the food is delicious. Whether it is his own creation, or a family favorite passed down through the generations, Chef Marco creates dishes that can be appreciated by all. Flavors can be subtle and mild, to bold and flavorful. It just depends on our mood. Cheen Hauye has it all.

¾ C. olive oil
¼ C. soy sauce
1 orange, cut in half
1 lemon, cut in half
1 lime , cut in half
2 bay leaves
12 black pepper-corns, toasted and crushed
½ bulb fennel, thinly sliced
½ red onion, thinly sliced
6 cloves garlic, thinly sliced
1 (1-inch) piece fresh ginger, peeled and thinly sliced
4 (8-oz.) boneless Mahi-Mahi fillets

1. Pour the olive oil and soy sauce into a large mixing bowl. Squeeze in the juice of the orange, lemon and lime, and toss in the squeezed rinds. Add the remaining ingredients and mix well.

2. Prepare the grill to medium.

3. Place the fish in the marinade and let sit for 10 minutes, turning once.

4. Remove the fish from the marinade and grill for 4 minutes on the first side and 2 minutes on the other side.

15400 Biscayne Boulevard, Miami, FL

Cheen Huaye

"I'll bet what motivated the British to colonize so much of the world is that they were just looking for a decent meal."
Martha Harrison

Irish Spring Roll

What it comes down to is this: it's all about the craic, banter, jokes, what ever you want to call it. Clarke's is more than just a bar and restaurant. We're a local, a pub, a joint. We're that place you come when your low, when your high, or when you just don't know. Try us. We're not always proper, but we're always serving it up. We're Irish brewed, Miami poured with New York attitude back.

2 C. finely diced corned beef
1 C. finely sliced cabbage
1 C. shredded potatoes
1 C. shredded pepper jack cheese
salt and pepper, to taste
5x5-inch egg roll wrappers
1 qt. oil

1. In a large mixing bowl, mix together corned beef, cabbage, potatoes and cheese. Season with salt and pepper.

2. Place 3 oz. of corned beef mixture into each egg roll wrapper and roll tightly. Seal edges with a brush of water and pinch closed.

3. Heat oil to 350°F.

4. Cook until egg rolls are golden brown. Drain on paper towels and serve.

840 1st Street, Miami Beach, FL

Clarke's

"Salt is born of the purest of parents: the sun and the sea."
Pythagoras

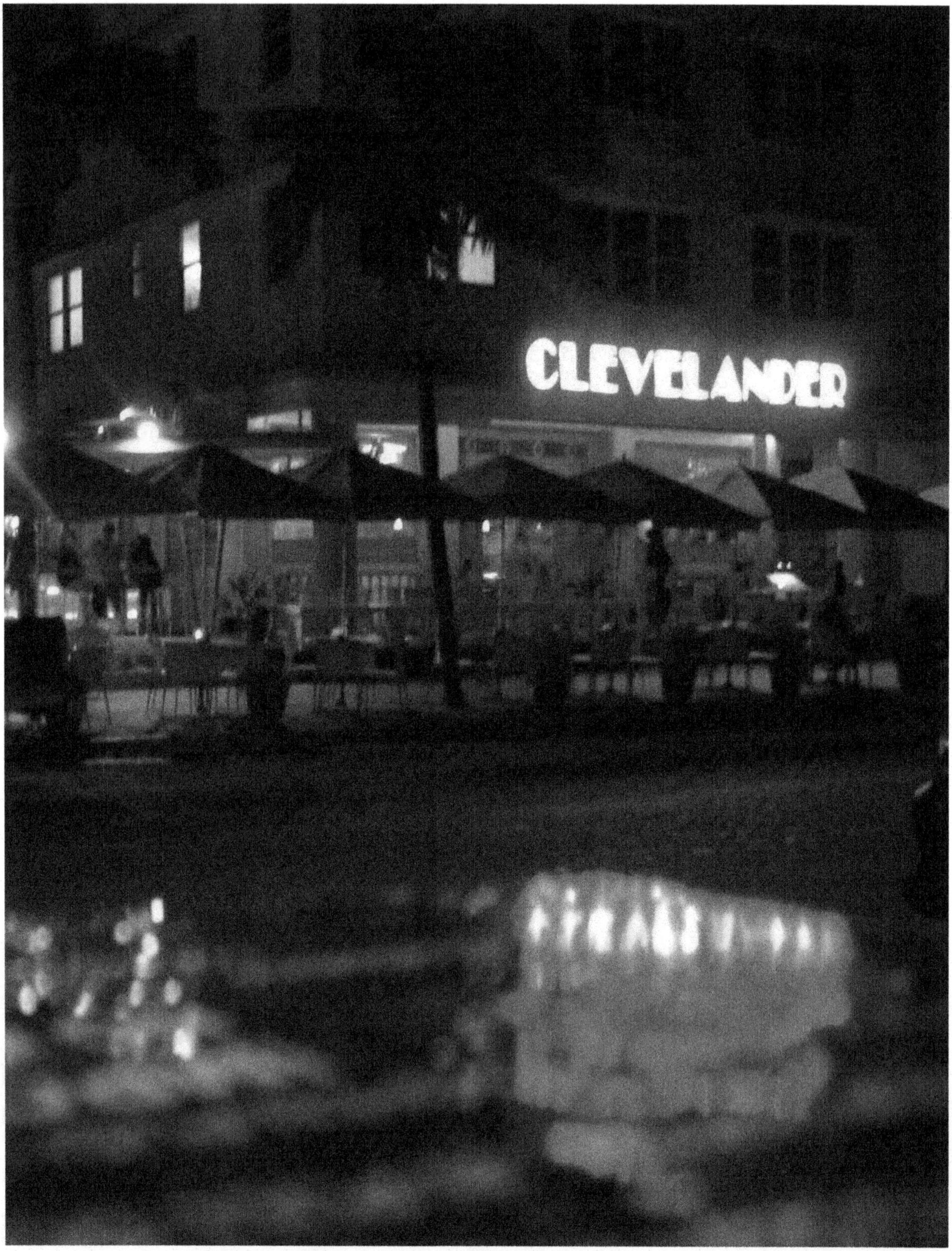
CLEVELANDER

Classic Eggs Benedict

A true icon amongst South Beach Miami hotels, restaurants, bars and entertainment venues. The Clevelander is back in action after a multi-million dollar renovation and upgrade to the ultimate one-stop destination experience. At the center of the Art Deco District on Ocean Drive, the Clevelander Hotel has expanded to include 60 revamped rooms and Rock-Star Suites, two rooftop decks with ocean-front and city views, enhanced poolside bars, a new café-style menu and its indoor music and dance venue – the 1020 music lounge.

2 large egg yolks
2 tsp. freshly squeezed lemon juice
1 C. (8 oz.) melted butter
pinch of salt
pinch of cayenne pepper
12 slices (⅛-inch thick) Canadian-style bacon

12 poached eggs
6 English muffins, split with a fork

For the Sauce:
1. Bring a saucepan of water to a simmer. In a non-reactive bowl, whisk together the egg yolks, lemon juice, and ½ tablespoon of water.

2. Place the bowl over the saucepan, making sure the bowl is not touching the water, and continue to whisk vigorously until ribbons form; be careful not to overheat the yolks or they will scramble.

3. Remove the bowl and slowly drizzle in the melted butter, continuing to whisk until the butter is absorbed into the mixture.

4. Add the salt and cayenne pepper.

5. Transfer to a ceramic serving bowl and keep on a warm place on the stove for up to 1 hour.

To Finish the Dish:
1. Place the split muffins on a large cookie sheet and toast under the broiler until golden brown.

2. Transfer the toasted muffins to warm serving plates and place one slice of the bacon on each muffin half.

3. Place a poached egg on top of the bacon and spoon the hollandaise over each egg.

1020 Ocean Drive, Miami Beach, FL

Clevelander

"In Mexico we have a word for sushi: bait."
Jose Simon

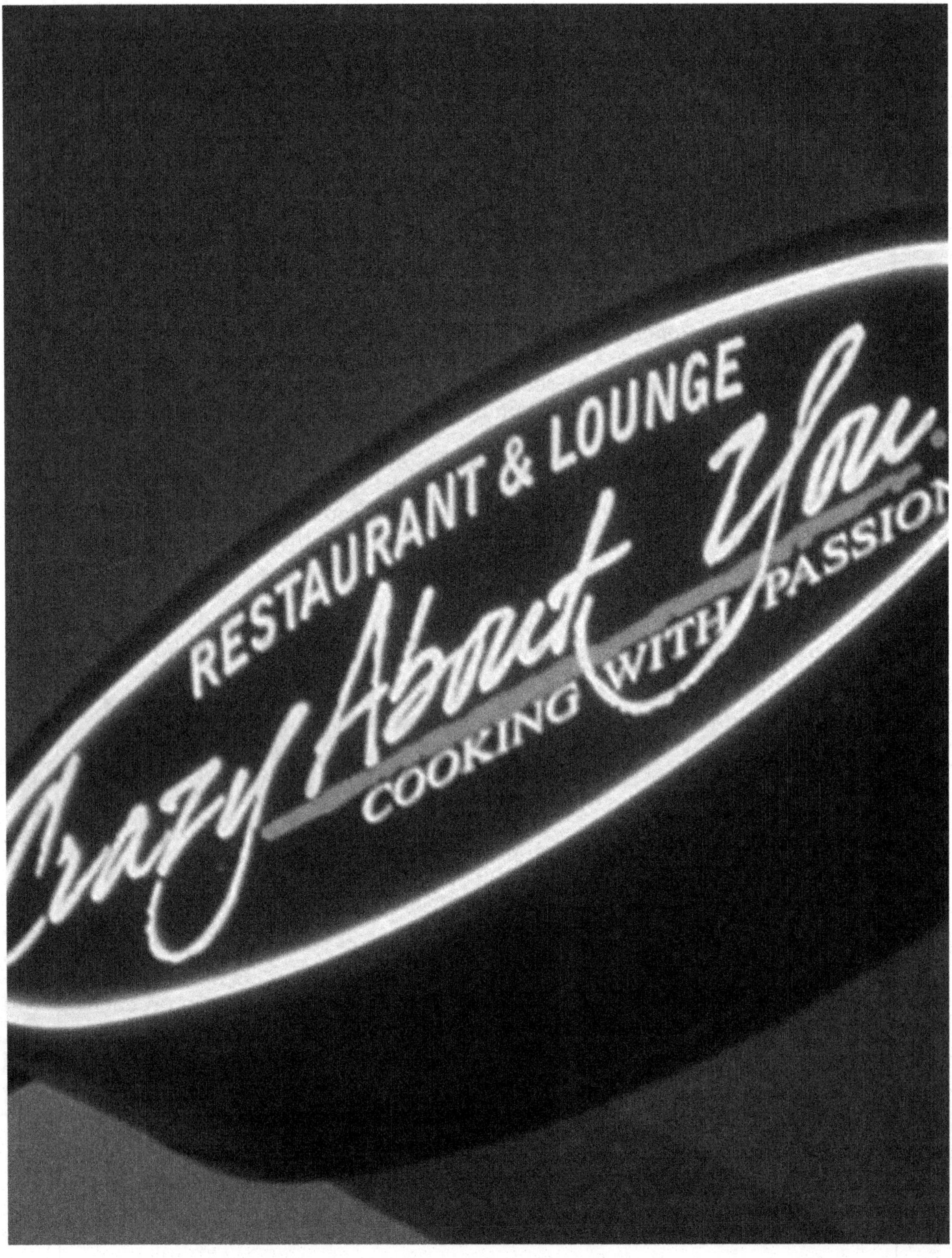
RESTAURANT & LOUNGE
Crazy About You
COOKING WITH PASSION

Lentil Soup

Signature Tastes of MIAMI

The newest concept for affordable dining in Brickell is Crazy About You. With it's truly unique lounge setting, warm décor, prestigious dining room, and picturesque waterfront dining, it is bound to be one of Brickell's most upscale preferred destinations. Whether you are dining with us and enjoying our romantic bay-front terrace or sampling cocktails in the lounge, listening to relaxing rhythms, Crazy About You is truly an experience not to be missed.

1 tbsp. oil 1 onion, chopped 2 carrots, chopped ¼ tsp. dried basil, marjoram, and rosemary 1 C. lentils 3 C. warm water 1 (14-oz.) can of crushed tomato 1 tbsp. cumin, or to taste 1 tsp. salt, or to taste	**1.** In a large soup pot, add 1 tbsp. of oil and sauté onion and carrots over medium heat until onions are soft. **2.** Add the dried herbs, stir and cook about 2 minutes. **3.** Add the lentils, stir and cook about 2 minutes more. **4.** Add the water, tomatoes, cumin, and salt. **5.** Cover and simmer until lentils are tender and soup has thickened slightly, about 45 minutes.

Crazy About You
1155 Brickell Bay Drive #101, Miami, FL

"Great restaurants are, of course, nothing but mouth-brothels. There is no point in going to them if one intends to keep one's belt buckled."
Frederic Raphael

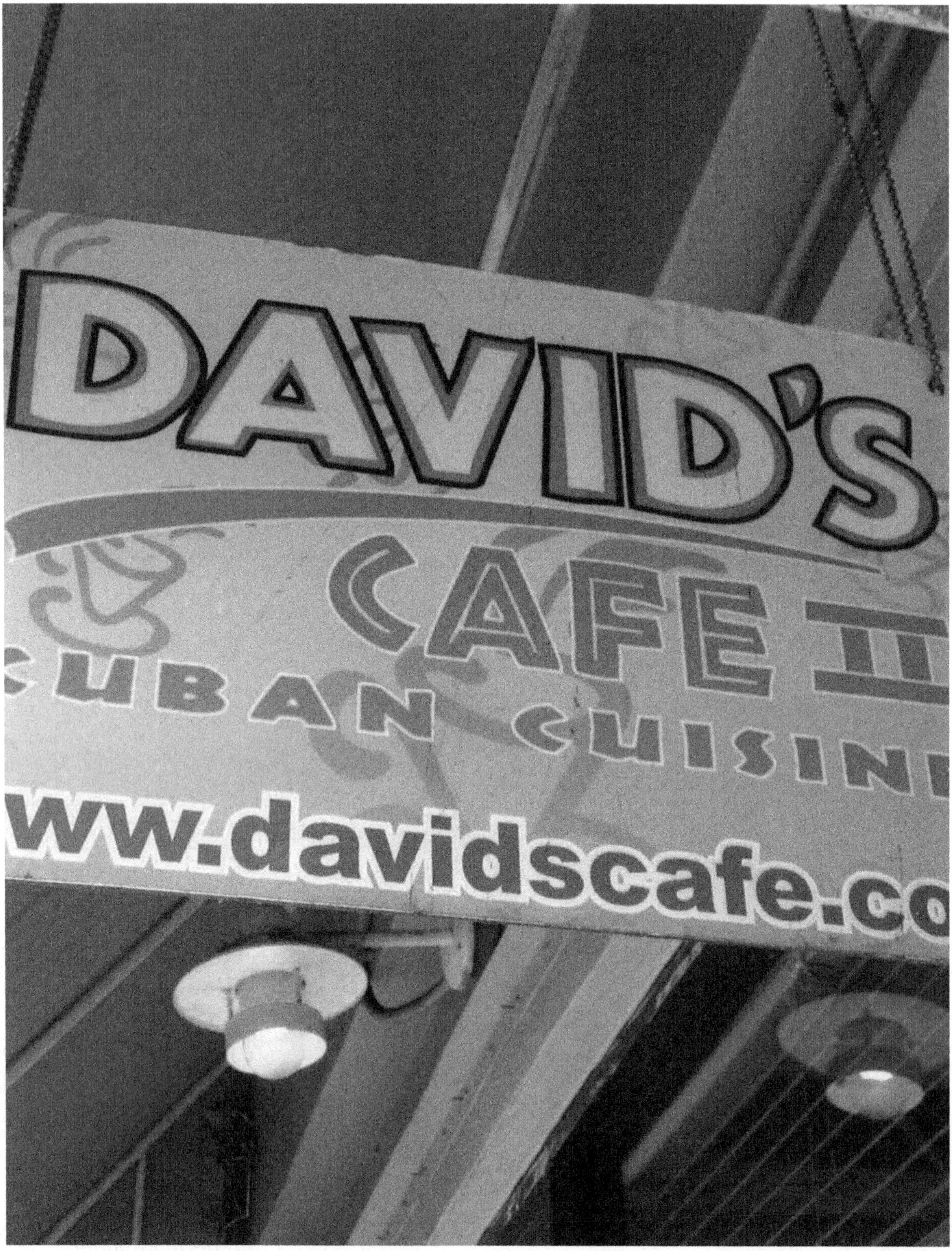
DAVID'S
CAFE II
CUBAN CUISIN
www.davidscafe.co

Masitas de Puerco

Signature Tastes of MIAMI

All the hard work has paid off and our dream became a Cuban-American institution; a place where two worlds came together. In 1993, when Lincoln Road was still finding its way, Alfredo and Maria opened David's Café II. Today the Gonzalez family keeps their dreams and traditions alive, as both restaurants are still family owned and operated for 33 years. We invite you to come and experience this family gem Cuban restaurant in the heart of the thriving South Beach.

2 lb. lean boneless pork (shoulder or leg), cut into 2-inch cubes
salt and freshly ground black pepper, to taste
4 garlic cloves, smashed
¼ C. orange juice
⅛ C. each fresh lime and lemon juice
vegetable oil or peanut oil, for frying

1. Sprinkle the meat liberally with salt and pepper.

2. Crush the garlic into a paste and rub the pork with the garlic paste. Place the pork in a nonreactive bowl and add the orange juice. Cover and refrigerate for 2 to 3 hours. Drain the pork cubes.

3. In a large saucepan heat 2 inches of oil until very hot but not smoking, then add the pork cubes, without crowding, working in batches if necessary. Raise the heat to high and brown the cubes, turning frequently with a slotted spoon until they are a rich, golden brown, about 10 minutes.

4. Transfer browned pork to a paper-towel-lined platter to drain; keep warm in a 200ºF oven until all the cubes are fried.

5. Serve immediately, with Moros y Cristianos (Black Beans and Rice) and Mojo Criollo (Creole Garlic Sauce).

1058 Collins Avenue, Miami Beach, FL

David's Café

"There is a communication of more than our bodies when bread is broken and wine is drunk. And that is my answer when people ask me: Why do you write about hunger, and not wars or love."
MFK Fisher

Pork Milanese

South Beach's chic Lincoln Road is lined with trendy restaurants, but from the moment you walk into De Luca, you'll be impressed with the welcoming atmosphere and gracious service. Grab a seat for some of the most delicious food you have ever tasted. While considering the menu, sip a nice wine from the carefully compiled list, including reds, whites, rosés and - bubblies at prices that won't bruise your budget.

1 garlic clove, minced
2 tbsp. fresh lemon juice
2 tbsp. extra virgin olive oil
coarse salt and ground pepper
1 C. all-purpose flour
1½ lb. pork cutlets (¼-inch thick)
2 tbsp. vegetable oil, plus more if needed
3 C. baby arugula
1 head radicchio or endive or a combination, thinly sliced
⅓ C. thinly sliced red onion

1. In a small bowl, whisk together garlic, lemon juice, and olive oil and season with salt and pepper; set dressing aside.

2. Place flour in a small bowl. Season pork with salt and pepper and dredge in flour, shaking off excess.

3. In a large skillet, heat vegetable oil over medium-high. When oil is hot, add cutlets, working in batches and adding more oil if necessary (do not overcrowd pan). Cook until cutlets are golden on bottom, 3 minutes. Flip and cook until cooked through, 3 minutes. Transfer cutlets to a large platter.

4. In a large bowl, toss arugula, radicchio, and onion with dressing, then top cutlets with salad.

530 Lincoln Road, Miami Beach, FL

De Luca

"The smell of good bread baking, like the sound of lightly flowing water, is indescribable in it's evocation of innocence and delight."
MFK Fisher

Chocolate Croquettes

The Godfather of Nuevo Latino Cuisine, Chef Douglas Rodriguez is a pioneer in the culinary world. With a number of award-winning restaurants around the country, best-selling cookbooks, and television appearances under his belt, Chef Douglas incorporates his highly regarded 'Nuevo Latino' cuisine into his latest sensation, DeRodriguez Cuba on Ocean. DeRod Cuba presents a new twist on classic dishes, delivering diners on South Beach an authentic experience to be remembered.

De Rodriguez Cuba on Ocean
101 Ocean Drive, Miami Beach, FL

*100 g whole milk
60 g heavy cream
185 g good-quality
bittersweet chocolate
45 g good-quality
milk chocolate
2 whole eggs, beate
100 g bread crumbs)
50 g dried coconut*

1. Chop the bittersweet and milk chocolates into small pieces and place in a bowl.

2. Boil the cream and milk together gently in a heavy based pan and then pour the hot liquid over the chocolate pieces.

3. Stir mixture until smooth. Cover and refrigerate until set.

4. Mix the bread crumbs and the coconut together in a small bowl. You can substitute hazelnut or almond powder instead of coconut.

5. When the chocolate mix has set, scoop small spoonfuls and then shape into balls by rolling gently between two hands.

6. Dip chocolate into the beaten eggs, then roll in the bread crumb and coconut mixture. Repeat twice or until croquettes are fully coated with crumbs (this will prevent them from bursting while cooking).

7. Heat a mild flavored oil to 350°F. Fry the croquettes for 30 seconds to 1 minute until lightly browned.

8. Serve immediately with coffee or vanilla ice cream.

"I prefer to regard a dessert as I would imagine the perfect woman: subtle, a little bittersweet, not blowsy and extrovert. Delicately made up, not highly rouged. Holding back, not exposing everything and, of course, with a flavor that lasts."
Graham Kerr

Warm Quiche Tray

Jahn Kirchoff and Mike Maler set out 22 years ago to open a restaurant that would serve top notch food at reasonable prices. With over 50 years of combined restaurant experience the two hoped Deli Lane would be the kind of place that people would want to visit over and over again and that would become a part of its community. Jahn had been compiling unique recipes for years during his travels around the US and abroad in the hopes of one day serving up these delicacies.

2 sheets reduced-fat puff pastry
1 tbsp. olive oil
1¼ C. button mushrooms, sliced
2 small carrots, grated
2 small zucchini, grated
3 C. broccoli florets
2 green onions, thinly sliced
5 eggs
¾ C. reduced-fat milk
1¼ C. reduced-fat cheese, grated

1. Preheat oven to 375°F. Place a baking sheet into the oven.

2. Line a 9-inch fluted quiche pan with the puff pastry and trim excess with a knife. Prick base several times with a fork. Place a sheet of parchment paper over pastry and fill halfway with dried beans or pie weights. Place pan onto hot baking sheet in the oven and blind bake for 10 minutes. Remove the beans and paper. Bake puff pastry shell another 10 minutes. Remove from oven and set aside.

3. Heat oil in a non-stick frying pan over medium-high heat. Add the mushrooms and sauté for 4 minutes. Add the remaining vegetables and cook for 2 minutes. Remove from heat and let cool.

4. Whisk the eggs and milk together in a bowl. Season with salt and pepper.

5. Spread the cooled vegetable mixture over the pastry shell. Sprinkle with grated cheese. Pour egg mixture over top.

6. Reduce oven to 350°F. Return quiche to hot baking sheet. Bake for 30 to 35 minutes or until set. Let stand for 10 minutes. Serve.

Deli Lane Café
1401 Brickell Avenue, Miami, FL

"A man taking basil from a woman will love her always."
Sir Thomas Moore

Wonton Soup

Chinese dim sum restaurant Chef Philip Ho debuted in Sunny Isles Beach a little more than a month ago, and already the name is burning on the tongues of local food trenders like too much Chinese mustard. Ho hit the social-network jackpot: Chowhounders, Yelpers, bloggers, and tweeters posted instant reviews, whose extrapolation would read like a rallying cry — Go to Ho!

4 C. reduced-sodium chicken stock 1-inch piece fresh ginger, peeled 1½ tbsp. soy sauce 5 oz. ground chicken (or pork) 2 tsp. cornflour ½ small carrot, grated ½ small zucchini, grated 2 button mushrooms, grated 2 tsp. finely chopped fresh chives 1 garlic clove, crushed 16 wonton wrappers chopped fresh chives, for garnish	**1.** Place the stock, ginger, 1 tablespoon soy sauce and 2 cups cold water in a large saucepan over medium heat. Cover and bring to a simmer. **2.** Meanwhile, gently combine ground chicken, cornflour, carrot, zucchini, mushrooms, chives, garlic, and remaining soy sauce in a bowl. **3.** Place 1 wonton wrapper on a cutting board. Place 1 heaped teaspoon of the mixture in center. Brush edges with water. Fold up sides to form a pouch. Pinch to close. Place on a plate. Repeat with remaining mixture and wrappers. **4.** Add wontons to simmering stock mixture. Cook, uncovered, for 5 to 7 minutes or until wontons are cooked through and float to the surface. **5.** Using a slotted spoon, transfer wontons to bowls. Remove and discard ginger from stock and ladle stock over the wontons. Sprinkle with chives. Serve.

Dim Sum at Chef Philip Ho
16850 Collins Ave, North Miami Beach, FL

"Cooking is like love, it should be entered into with abandon or not at all."
Harriet Van Horne, Vogue

Sapphire Collins

Originally built in 1923, our restaurant was once the site of Miami's Fire Station No. 4, built in the popular Mediterranean Revival style of the era at that time. The Architect, H. Hasting Mundy, built this classic design with a two-story hipped roof, arcaded porch, stucco walls, and unique balconies. This whimsical building is now listed on the National Register of Historic Places. Located in the heart of Brickell's Financial District, our restaurant, which opened October of 2007, offers a unique selection of International fusion cuisine.

1½ oz. Bombay Sapphire gin
¾ oz. simple syrup
½ oz. fresh lemon juice
4 bing cherries, pitted
8 blueberries
club soda
1 bing cherry, for garnish
lemon wheel, for garnish

1. In a collins glass, muddle the blueberries and cherries in the lemon juice and simple syrup.

2. Add Bombay Sapphire gin and ice and stir briefly.

3. Top with club soda.

4. Garnish with a lemon wheel and bing cherry.

Dolores But You Can Call Me Lolita
1000 South Miami Avenue, Miami, FL

"To give life to beauty, the painter uses a whole range of colours, musicians of sounds, the cook of tastes—and it is indeed remarkable that there are seven colours, seven musical notes and seven tastes."
Lucien Tendret (1825-1896) 'La Table au pays de Brillat-Savarin'

Salmon Carpaccio

Signature Tastes of MIAMI

Doraku, the brainchild of Kevin Aoki — son of legendary Benihana founder Rocky Aoki — already serves the best sushi in South Beach in one of the most chill settings, a sumptuously lit maze of birdcages and deeply recessed booths.

8 oz. very fresh king salmon fillet, skin and pin bones removed
1 tbsp. olive oil
1 C. chiffonade endive
¼ C. finely chopped red onions
¼ C. extra virgin olive oil
1 tsp. chopped parsley
1 tsp. chopped chives
2 tbsp. lemon juice
1 tsp. lemon zest
fresh cracked black pepper
sea salt

1. Cut the salmon into 4 equal portions. Cover a cutting board with a large piece of plastic wrap and rub with 1 teaspoon of the olive oil. Place a piece of salmon in the center and cover with a second piece of plastic.

2. Using a flat, smooth mallet or the bottom of a skillet, gently pound the salmon into a paper-thin sheet. Transfer to a plate. Repeat with the remaining salmon, adding more oil as necessary to prevent sticking. Lightly season each piece of salmon with pepper and sea salt.

3. In a small bowl, combine the endive and red onions. In another bowl, combine the extra virgin olive oil, parsley, chives, lemon juice and lemon zest, and whisk to blend. Season with sea salt and black pepper. Toss 2 tablespoons of the vinaigrette with the endive and red onions.

4. Place about ¼ cup of the endive and red onion salad in the center of each piece of salmon. Drizzle the remaining vinaigrette over the salmon, and serve well chilled.

1104 Lincoln Road, Miami Beach, FL

Doraku

"When you wake up in the morning, Pooh,' said Piglet at last, 'what's the first thing you say to yourself?' 'What's for breakfast?' said Pooh. 'What do you say, Piglet?' 'I say, I wonder what's going to happen exciting today?' said Piglet. Pooh nodded thoughtfully. 'It's the same thing,' he said."
A. A. Milne, 'The House at Pooh Corner'

El Mago de las Fritas

oted best Frita in Mia

Split Pea Soup

A big welcome from El Mago. Please browse the great Frita Menu that has been enjoyed by guests from all over Miami, Florida, and the world. When you sink your teeth into El Mago's Frita Cubana (Cuban hamburger), the Pan con Bistec (steak sandwich) or try one of his incredible Batidos (shakes) you will see why El Mago has been a staple of South Florida guests and residents. So again welcome to our kitchen, we are glad to have you as our guest of honor.

2 tbsp. (¼ stick) butter
1 large onion, chopped
1 C. chopped celery
1 C. chopped peeled carrots
1½ lb. smoked pork hocks
2 tsp. dried leaf marjoram
1½ C. green split peas
8 C. water

1. Melt butter in a heavy, large pot or Dutch oven over medium-high heat. Add onion, celery and carrots. Sauté until vegetables begin to soften, about 8 minutes. Add pork and marjoram; stir 1 minute.

2. Add the peas, then water, and bring to boil. Reduce heat to medium-low. Partially cover and simmer soup until pork and vegetables are tender and peas are falling apart, stirring often, about 1 hour and 10 minutes.

3. Transfer hocks to bowl. Puree 5 cups of the soup in batches in a blender. Return to pot. Cut pork off bones. Dice pork; return pork to soup. Season with salt and pepper.

Note: Can be made 1 day ahead. Refrigerate until cold, then cover. Rewarm before serving.

El Mago De Las Fritas
5828 Southwest 8th Street, Miami, FL

"How do they taste? They taste like more."
H.L. Mencken

Shrimp Casino

Signature Tastes of MIAMI

Over two decades ago a group of Nicaraguan friends living in Miami decided to create a restaurant that would feature the finest Nicaraguan dishes in an ambiance representative of its Spanish-colonial architecture. It would be a place where people would be exposed to the Nicaraguan traditions of fine cuisine, personalized service and festive entertainment. In 1985 El Novillo Restaurant came to fruition and thus a Nicaraguan home was transformed into the premier Latin steakhouse.

1 lb. large shrimp (16-20 count), cleaned and peeled
2 slices bacon, cut into small pieces
4 cloves garlic, crushed
¼ C. roasted red peppers
dash of red pepper flakes
olive oil, to coat pan
½ C. white wine
loaf of crusty Italian bread

1. In a large pan, fry the bacon and garlic over medium heat until bacon is cooked, but not too crisp, and garlic is lightly browned.

2. Add enough olive oil to coat the bottom of the pan then add the red pepper flakes and roasted peppers. Add in the shrimp.

3. Once shrimp turn pink on one side, pour in the white wine and turn shrimp over to finish cooking. Do not overcook shrimp.

4. Pour shrimp and sauce into large bowl and serve with crusty Italian bread.

El Novillo Restaurant
15450 New Barn Road #110, Miami Lakes, FL

"There is no love sincerer than the love of food."
George Bernard Shaw

Mexican Ceviche

El Vato specializes in authentic Mexican cuisine! All of our meats are Humane Grade and we offer several vegetarian and vegan substitutes. We also carry over 60 brands of Tequila. Happy Hour is the best in Brickell and runs Monday-Friday 12 pm-8 pm. We also have Ladies Night on Wednesdays and offer all Chicas complimentary Margaritas!

1¼ lb. very fresh (sushi-grade) fish fillets (such as tuna, hamachi, barramundi, or mahi-mahi), cut into ½-inch cubes
fine sea salt
freshly ground black pepper
3 tbsp. fresh lime juice
2 tbsp. fresh lemon juice
2 tsp. sugar
1 C. chopped seeded tomatoes
¾ C. chopped red onion
2 tbsp. sliced pickled jalapeño chiles from a jar plus 1 tbsp. of their liquid
1 tbsp. olive oil
½ large head of romaine lettuce, very thinly sliced crosswise (3-4 C.)
1 large avocado, peeled, pitted, diced
3 tbsp. chopped fresh cilantro
12 crisp taco shells
salsa

1. Place fish in a medium glass dish or bowl; sprinkle with sea salt and freshly ground black pepper. Add lime juice, lemon juice, and sugar and toss. Cover and chill until fish turns white and no longer looks raw, tossing occasionally, at least 4 hours and up to 6 hours.

2. Strain fish; discard marinade. Place ceviche in a large bowl; add the tomatoes, red onion, pickled jalapeños, 1 tablespoon of their liquid from the jar, and olive oil and toss to blend.

3. Add lettuce, avocado, and cilantro to ceviche mixture and toss.

4. Fill taco shells with ceviche mixture. Top each taco with a large spoonful of salsa and serve.

El Vato Tequila and Taco Bar
1010 South Miami Avenue, Miami, FL

"Of all the items on the menu, soup is that which exacts the most delicate perfection and the strictest attention."
Escoffier

Potato Skins

This roadside gem boasts a simple menu, casual atmosphere, and fair share of beer and wine. Family owned and operated, Elwoods has plenty of personality, delicious fish and chips, succulent burgers, and great desserts. Less-is-more mentality is definitely at play at Elwoods, and it's not a bad thing. Simple design and layout make you feel right at home, allowing the food and drink to take center stage.

6 small to medium russet baking potatoes (total 3 lb.)
olive oil, canola oil, or grapeseed oil
Kosher salt
freshly ground pepper
6 strips of bacon
4 oz. grated cheddar cheese
½ C. sour cream
2 green onions, thinly sliced, white and green parts

1. Preheat oven to 400°F. Scrub the potatoes then rub with olive oil and bake for 1 hour or until the potatoes are cooked through. (You can also microwave the potatoes on high for about 5 minutes per potato.)

2. While the potatoes are cooking, cook the bacon strips in a frying pan set over medium-low heat for 10 to 15 minutes, or until crisp. Drain bacon on paper towels, let cool, then crumble.

3. Remove the potatoes from the oven and let cool. Cut in half horizontally. Use a spoon to carefully scoop out the insides, reserving the scooped potatoes for another use, leaving about ¼ of an inch of potato on the skin.

4. Increase the oven to 450°F. Brush grapeseed oil or canola oil over the potato skins, inside and out. Sprinkle with salt. Place potato skins on a baking rack in a roasting pan and bake for 10 minutes on one side, then flip the skins over and bake for another 10 minutes. Remove from oven and let cool. Preheat the broiler.

5. Arrange the potato skins skin-side down on the roasting pan or rack. Sprinkle the insides with freshly ground black pepper, cheddar cheese, and crumbled bacon. Return to the oven. Broil for an additional 2 minutes, or until the cheese is bubbly. Remove from oven. Use tongs to place skins on a serving plate. Add a dollop of sour cream to each skin and sprinkle with green onions. Serve hot.

Elwoods Gastro Pub
188 NE 3rd Ave, Miami, FL

"There are many miracles in the world to be celebrated and, for me, garlic is the most deserving."
Leo Buscaglia

81

Rustic Tomato and Onion Salad

Since being founded in 1945 the Epicure Market has consistently and continually competed with the world's finest gourmet markets. Originally started by the Thal family, the small store on Alton Road in Miami Beach grew ever popular since its inception right after World War II. Starting out as a butcher shop the store slowly developed other areas such as produce and gourmet groceries. The entire family pitched in and started cooking using recipes that are still being used today.

4 large firm tomatoes
1 medium white onion
1 clove garlic, crushed
1 handful of black olives
3 tbsp. extra virgin olive oil
1 tbsp. lemon juice or white wine vinegar
1 tsp. sweet basil and rosemary leaf tips, finely chopped

1. Combine oil and lemon juice or vinegar, and garlic. Set aside.

2. Slice tomatoes and onion, put on a shallow platter or flat dish and chill 20-30 minutes.

3. To serve, add olives, shake dressing and pour over top.

Epicure Gourmet Market
1656 Alton Road, Miami Beach, FL

"Leave the gun. Take the cannolis."
Clemenza, in The Godfather

Crunchy Spiced Chickpeas

Escopazzo opened its doors in 1993 with only 35 seats, the charming restaurant had later expanded adding a second room and creating a perfect setting for private parties; increasing its capacity to accommodate a total of 90. A stone fountain and a quaint sitting bar dress this warm space, reminiscent of a Tuscan courtyard. The "climate control wine cellar" becomes the focal point for this private dining area; housing an "Italian only" Wine Spectator Award Winning collection of more than 400 different labels.

Escopazzo Organic Italian
1311 Washington Avenue, Miami Beach, FL

2 (15-oz.) cans chickpeas
extra virgin olive oil
1 tbsp. ground smoked spanish paprika (sweet or hot, if hot, reduce cayenne by half)
1 tsp. ground cayenne pepper
Kosher salt

1. Line a large baking sheet with parchment paper. Set aside.

2. Line a second baking sheet with a clean kitchen towel or several layers of paper towel. Pour both cans of chickpeas into a meshed strainer or colander and rinse well under cold running water.

3. Let drain for 5 minutes in the strainer, then pour chickpeas onto the towel-lined baking sheet and spread out evenly. Leave to dry on the counter for 1 hour. At 30 minutes before roasting, preheat oven to 425°F.

4. Place the chickpeas on the parchment-lined baking sheet and roast for approximately 30 to 40 minutes, shaking the pan every 10 minutes so that they cook evenly. When done, the chickpeas will be crisp, golden, and have shrunken slightly.

5. Once crisp, remove from the oven and drizzle with olive oil (about 1 to 2 tablespoons), sprinkle with the spices and season with Kosher salt. Toss to coat evenly and serve.

"A jazz musician can improvise based on his knowledge of music. He understands how things go together. For a chef, once you have that basis, that's when cuisine is truly exciting."
Charlie Trotter

Cajun Style Fries

In 1986 Jerry and Janie Murrell offered sage advice to the four young Murrell brothers: "Start a business or go to college." The business route won and the Murrell family opened a carry-out burger joint in Alexandria, Virginia. During the 1980's and 1990's the Murrell family perfected their simple system. Five Guys was The Place to get a fresh, juicy burger with all the toppings you could stuff between fresh-baked buns.

4 medium potatoes
¼ tsp. oregano
¼ tsp. thyme
1 tsp. paprika
⅛ tsp. cayenne (or to taste)
⅛ tsp. black pepper
¼ tsp. sugar
¼ tsp. cumin
½ tsp. salt
1 tsp. garlic powder
½ tsp. onion powder
¼ tsp. Tabasco sauce
1 tbsp. vegetable oil

1. Preheat oven to 400°F. In a small bowl, combine oregano, thyme, paprika, cayenne, black pepper, sugar, cumin, salt, garlic powder, onion powder, Tabasco sauce, and oil; mix well into a paste.

2. Line a large baking sheet with aluminum foil; pour a small amount of oil onto foil and spread with a paper towel. Peel potatoes and cut into french fry shapes.

3. Place fries in a plastic bag with paste and work paste onto fries; alternatively you can do this in a bowl, but the bag method is easier. Place fries on lined baking sheet, trying not to let edges touch.

4. Bake in oven for approximately 30-35 minutes (time may vary with the size fry you cut); turn once during cooking to brown underside.

Five Guys Burgers and Fries
3401 North Miami Avenue, Miami, FL

"He that but looketh on a plate of ham and eggs to lust after it hath already committed breakfast in his heart."
C. S. Lewis

Chocolate Ecstasy

Flanigan's has been around for over 50 years, and any business that has been around that long has got to be doing something right. They are famous for their legendary Baby Back Ribs (considered by most who taste them as the best Baby Backs on the planet!), and they sell over a million pounds a year. Also known for their fresh fish, and have several different preparation options for their fresh Mahi-Mahi and fresh Tuna. You cannot get fresher fish unless you catch it yourself!

Signature Tastes of MIAMI

Flanigan's Seafood Bar & Grill

2721 Bird Ave, Miami, FL

Cake:
4 oz. semisweet chocolate
½ C. unsalted butter
1 C. finely chopped pecans
2 large eggs, lightly beaten
2 C. granulated sugar
1½ all-purpose flour
1 tsp. baking powder
½ tsp. salt
1½ C. milk
1 tsp. vanilla extract

Chocolate Filling:
4 oz semisweet chocolate
¼ C. unsalted butter
½ C. sifted confectioners' sugar
⅓ C. milk

Chocolate Frosting:
2 C. heavy whipping cream
1 C. sifted powdered sugar
⅔ C. sifted cocoa
1 tsp. vanilla extract

Cake:
1. Preheat oven to 350°F.
2. Grease and flour two 9-inch round cake pans. Set aside.
3. Combine chocolate and butter in the top of a double boiler. Bring water to a boil. Reduce heat to low and stir until chocolate melts.
4. Add pecans and stir well. Remove from heat.
5. Combine eggs and sugar in a large mixing bowl. Beat at high speed until thickened and pale.
6. Stir in chocolate mixture.
7. Combine flour, baking powder, and salt. Add to chocolate mixture alternately with milk, beginning and ending with flour.
8. Stir in vanilla. Pour batter into prepared pans.
9. Bake for 45-48 minutes or until inserted toothpick comes out clean.
10. Cool layers in pans for 5 minutes then turn out onto wire racks. Cool completely.

Filling:
1. Combine chocolate and butter in the top of a double boiler. Bring water to a boil. Reduce heat and stir until chocolate melts.
2. Gradually add powdered sugar, altenatively with milk, beginning and ending with sugar.
3. Stir until smooth. Cover and chill for 30 minutes or until mixture reaches spreading consistency.
4. Spread filling between cake layers.

Frosting:
1. Combine all ingredients in a bowl.
2. Beat at high speed until stiff peaks form.
3. Chill 30 minutes.
4. Frost sides and top of cake.
5. Refrigerate until ready to serve. Store leftovers in the refrigerator.

"To be tempted and indulged by the city's most brilliant chefs. It's the dream of every one of us in love with food."
Gael Greene

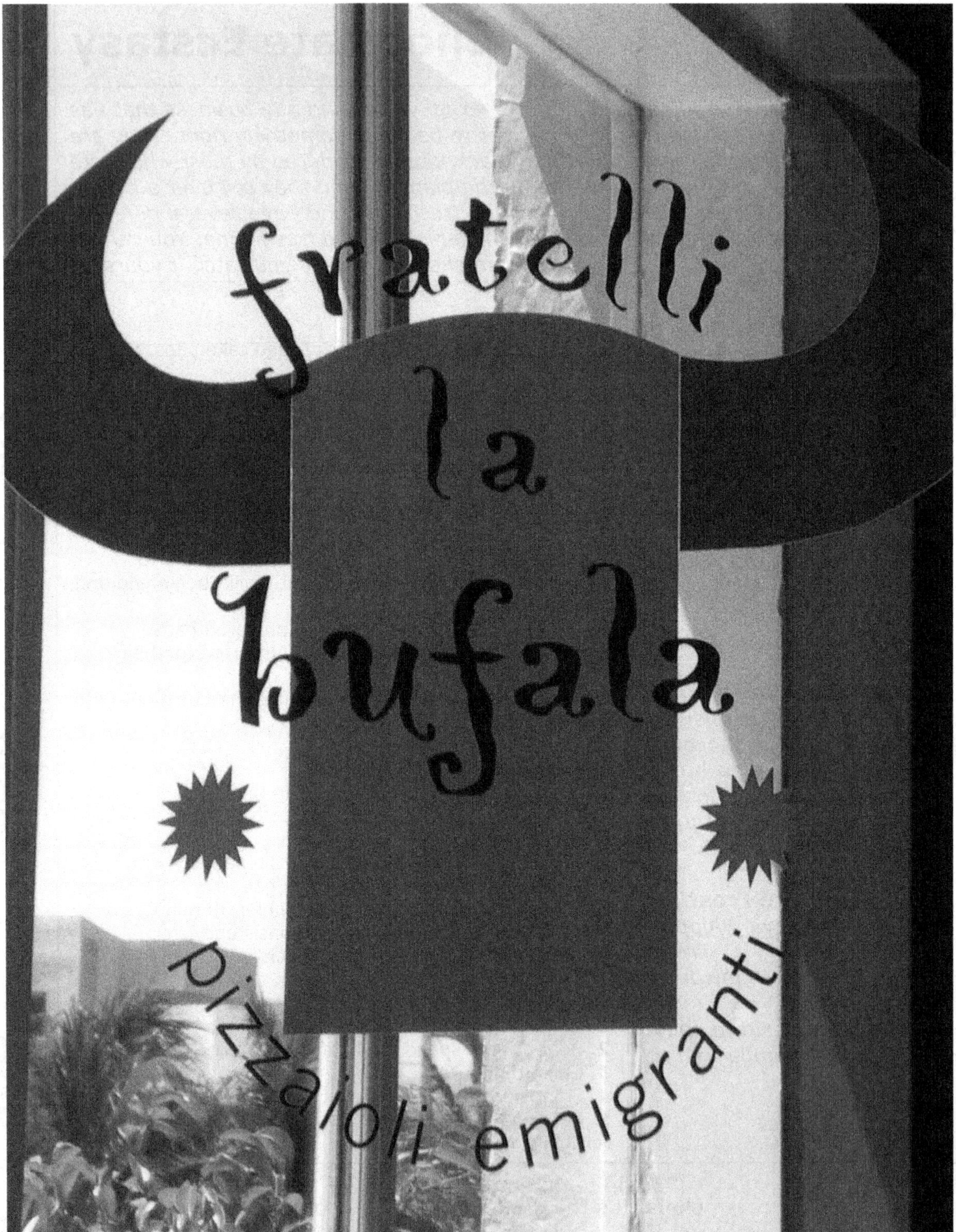
fratelli
la
bufala
pizzaioli emigranti

Signature Tastes of MIAMI

In 2000, Gennaro decided to open a pizza restaurant in Milan as well, but without giving up on painting. The three brothers retrieved their father's business creating a company and in 2003 they give life to the Fratelli La Bufala brand. Gennaro kept on painting and some of his masterpieces are now on display in FLB restaurants all over the world.

2 C. chickpeas, soaked for 12 hours in plenty of cold water and drained
6 tbsp. olive oil
2 onions, finely chopped
2 carrots, finely diced
2 sticks celery, thinly sliced
3 tbsp. very finely chopped rosemary
4 cloves garlic, finely chopped
4 zucchini, diced
3 (15-oz.) cans whole Italian tomatoes, crushed
4 tbsp. tomato paste
1 C. water
salt and freshly ground black pepper
extra virgin olive oil, for serving

1. Place the chickpeas in a large pan of water. Bring to a boil, reduce heat then simmer until the chickpeas are tender (up to 1 hour). Drain well and toss with 2 tablespoons of the olive oil. Reserve until ready to use.

2. Heat the remaining 4 tablespoons of olive oil over moderate heat in a large pan and add the onions, carrots, celery, rosemary, garlic and zucchini. Fry gently without browning for 10 minutes or until the onion is soft.

3. Add cooked chickpeas, tomatoes and tomato paste, and water. Bring to a boil, reduce heat, and simmer for 30 minutes or until the soup is thick and creamy. Season with salt and pepper.

4. Serve soup drizzled with extra virgin olive oil.

Fratelli la Bufala

437 Washington Ave, Miami Beach, FL

"Great food is like great sex. The more you have the more you want."
Gael Greene

Grilled Flank Steak

Mr. Daniel Gonzalez, owner of the French Bistro developed expertise for Italian Cuisine while toiling in an Italian restaurant. He returned to his roots while managing the Argentinean Steak House "Rincon Argentino" in Coral Gables. Today, he and his wife Mabel broaden their culinary knowledge to bring fresh and innovating flavors to the community with their own restaurant offerings of the French Bistro.

1 (2-lb.) flank steak, trimmed
2 tsp. Worcestershire sauce
½ tsp. sea salt
½ tsp. freshly-ground black pepper
cooking spray

1. Place flank steak in an 11x7-inch baking dish. Sprinkle each side evenly with half of Worcestershire sauce, salt, and pepper; rub mixture into steak. Cover and refrigerate at least 20 minutes.

2. Prepare grill to high heat.

3. Place steak on grill rack coated with cooking spray; grill 8 minutes on each side over medium-high heat, or until desired degree of doneness.

4. Remove steak from grill and place on a cutting board; cover loosely with foil. Let stand 10 minutes. Cut steak diagonally across the grain into thin slices.

13611 S Dixie Hwy # 110, Miami, FL

French Bistro

"The Italians were eating with forks when the French were still eating each other."
Mario Batali

French Toast

Since 1990, The Front Porch Café has delivered your neighborhood "home away from home" dining experience right in the heart of South Beach to local residents and tourists alike. Our commitment is to always serve fresh food in generous portions at a reasonable price, making us the "Best Value on South Beach" (Miami New Times). We shop daily for the best available ingredients and use organic products where it is most feasible.

Signature Tastes of MIAMI

4 eggs
⅔ C. milk
2 tsp. of cinnamon
8 thick slices of
2-day-old bread
unsalted butter
maple syrup, optional
2 tsp. freshly grated
orange zest
¼ C. triple sec
fresh berries

1. Beat eggs, milk, and cinnamon together in a shallow bowl. Add orange zest and triple sec. Whisk until well blended.

2. Dip each slice of bread into the egg mixture, allowing bread to soak up some of the mixture.

3. Melt butter over medium-high heat in a large skillet. Add as many slices of bread into the skillet as will fit without crowding. Fry until brown on both sides, flipping the bread once.

4. Serve hot with more butter, maple syrup, and fresh berries.

Front Porch Café
1458 Ocean Drive, Miami Beach, FL

"It's bizarre that the produce manager is more important to my children's health than the pediatrician."
Meryl Streep

Toro Tartar

Signature Tastes of MIAMI

It's a place where you can enjoy a salad with homemade dressing or a go-go pie filled with nutella and banana. We offer choices for any palate whether your passion is Philly cheese steak or pan-seared tofu. Everything is made on-premises using premium, fresh ingredients. The attention is personal, the trappings are no-fuss. Insofar as possible, our prices are set for the everyday customer.

3¾ lb. very fresh tuna steak
1¼ C. olive oil
5 limes, zest grated
1 C. freshly squeezed lime juice
2½ tsp. wasabi powder
2½ tbsp. soy sauce
2 tbsp. hot red pepper sauce
2½ tbsp. Kosher salt
1½ tbsp. freshly ground black pepper
1¼ C. minced scallions, white and green parts (12 scallions)
3¼ tbsp. minced fresh jalapeño pepper, seeds removed
5 ripe Hass avocados
1½ tbsp. toasted sesame seeds, optional

1. Cut the tuna into ¼-inch dice and place it in a very large bowl.

2. In a separate bowl, combine the olive oil, lime zest, lime juice, wasabi, soy sauce, hot red pepper sauce, salt, and pepper.

3. Pour mixture over the tuna, add the scallions and jalapeño, and mix well. Cut the avocados in half, remove the seed, and peel. Cut the avocados into ¼-inch dice. Carefully mix the avocado into the tuna mixture.

4. Add the toasted sesame seeds, if using, and season to taste. Allow the mixture to sit in the refrigerator for at least 1 hour for the flavors to blend. Serve on crackers.

Go-Go Fresh Food Café
926 Alton Rd, Miami Beach, FL

"New York is the greatest city in the world for lunch ... That's the gregarious time. And when that first martini hits the liver like a silver bullet, there is a sigh of contentment that can be heard in Dubuque."
William Emerson Jr.

Gordon Biersch
DUNKLES
Gordon Biersch
BREWERY·RESTAURANT

Vegetable Stir Fry

Signature Tastes of MIAMI

2 tbsp. extra virgin olive oil
1 carrot, chopped
½ C. frozen green peas
¼ C. yellow or white onion, chopped
2 C. jasmine rice
¼ tsp. saffron threads
1 C. hot water
1¾ C. vegetable broth
1 tsp. Kosher salt

1. Place saffron threads in hot water and allow to bloom.

2. In a heavy sauce pan or "caldero" heat the extra virgin olive oil over medium heat and add carrots, onion, and green peas. Sauté for about 3 minutes until onion is translucent.

3. Add rice and sauté for about 2 minutes. Add water-saffron mixture, vegetable broth, and salt.

4. Turn heat to high and bring to a boil. Turn heat to low, cover, and cook until rice is done, about 17 minutes. Leave covered for 10 minutes before serving.

Gordon Biersch
1201 Brickell Avenue, Miami, FL

Smoked Butternut Squash Soup

This family-owned business has called Miami home for over 20 years, opening its first location on the renowned Bird Road in 1991. The story of the Graziano's family is the story of the aspiring Argentine immigrant that relocated to the United States in search of a brighter and better future. Through hard work and dedication, Mario Graziano and family made their dream a reality.

4 lbs. butternut squash, halved and cut into large chunks
3 strips bacon, diced
1 onion, diced
2 Granny Smith apples, diced
1 C. apple juice
⅛ C. white-wine vinegar
1½ qts. chicken stock
1 C. heavy cream
1 cinnamon stick
8 springs fresh thyme

1. Smoke butternut squash in a Cookshack smoker for about 30 minutes.

2. Preheat oven to 350°F. Place squash on a baking sheet and bake until soft and tender, about 10 to 15 minutes. Remove from oven, scoop out tender flesh and mash.

3. In a large soup pot, sauté bacon until it releases some of its fat, add the apples and onions and sauté until the onions are translucent.

4. Add apple juice and white-wine vinegar and reduce until almost dry. Add chicken stock, mashed squash pulp, and cinnamon stick. Bring to a boil and simmer, uncovered, for 20 minutes.

5. Add heavy cream and strain through a fine sieve.

6. Add thyme springs and steep for 30 minutes. Strain again and serve.

177 Southwest 7th Street, Miami, FL

Graziano's

"Food without wine is a corpse; wine without food is a ghost; united and well mitched they are as body and soul, living partners."
Andre Simon (1877-1970)

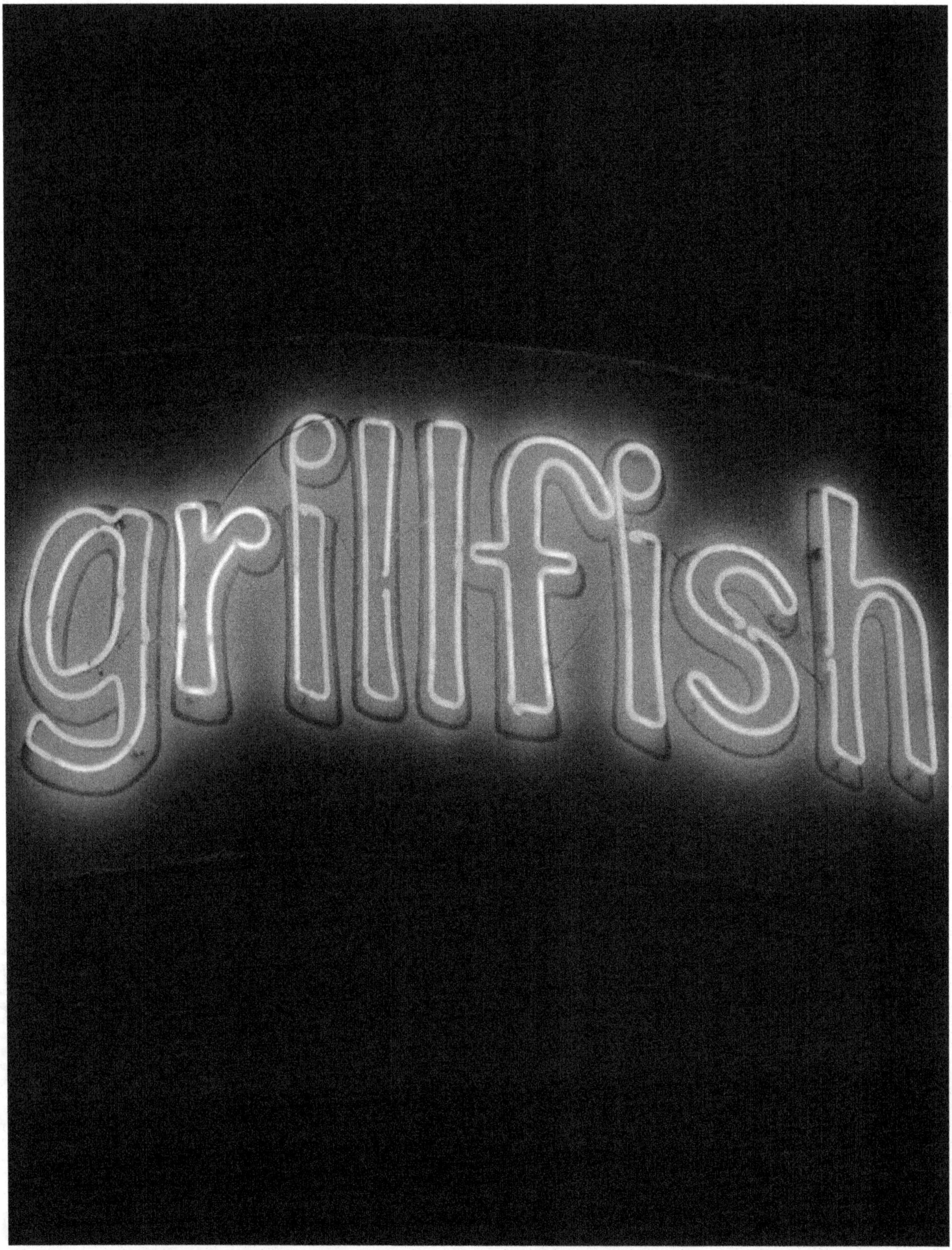
grillfish

Brownie Sundae

Grillfish is a casual, moderately-priced restaurant, specializing in fresh, grilled seafood, deliciously-sauced pasta and now serving up South Beach's best steak and chops. The restaurant is dominated by its "signature" oversized, floor-to-ceiling, erotic mural extending the entire wall behind the large stone bar. A definite conversation piece. The bars are ornately decorated with massive mirrors, large columns and a multitude of glowing candles.

Brownies:
½ C. (1 stick) unsalted butter, at room temperature, plus more for greasing the pan
3 oz. bittersweet chocolate, coarsely chopped
¾ C. granulated sugar
1 tsp. pure vanilla extract
3 large eggs
½ C. all-purpose flour

Caramel Sauce:
1 C. granulated sugar
½ C. heavy cream
1 tsp. pure vanilla extract

For Serving:
1 pint good-quality vanilla ice cream
½ C. pecan pieces

1. Preheat oven to 350°F. Butter an 8x8-inch baking dish.

2. In a heat-proof glass bowl, add the chocolate and cover with plastic wrap and microwave at 30-second intervals until just melted; stir well after each interval. Or bring about 1 inch of water to a simmer in the bottom of a double boiler or in a saucepan with a bowl that nests without touching the water. Put the chocolate in the top of the double boiler or in the bowl and stir until chocolate is melted, 2 to 3 minutes; remove from heat and set aside.

3. In a mixing bowl, beat the butter with the sugar until creamy and light colored. Add the melted chocolate and the vanilla and stir until smooth.

4. In a small bowl beat the eggs. Pour the eggs into the chocolate mixture and blend well. Stir in flour.

5. Pour the batter into the prepared baking dish and bake on the middle rack until a knife inserted into the center of the brownies comes out with moist crumbs attached, 30 to 35 minutes. Let cool about 10 minutes.

6. While the brownies bake, make the caramel sauce. Put the sugar and ½ cup water in a non-stick saucepan over low heat. Cook, stirring, until the sugar is dissolved, 1 to 2 minutes.

7. Turn the heat to medium and cook without stirring until the liquid turns a caramel color, about 20 minutes. Swirl the pan for even cooking.

8. When the syrup has turned a dark amber color, remove from the heat and immediately pour in the cream. Stand back—the caramel will splatter. Stir to combine. Return to low heat to melt the caramel and cook until smooth. Remove from heat and stir in the vanilla.

9. In the warm oven, spread the pecans on a baking sheet and toast until fragrant, about 10 minutes.

10. To serve, cut four 4-inch brownies and put them in a shallow bowl, add a couple of scoops of ice cream. Pour some of the caramel sauce over and sprinkle with the pecans.

1444 Collins Avenue, Miami Beach, FL

Grillfish

"After a good dinner one can forgive anybody, even one's own relatives."
Oscar Wilde

Passion Fruit Mousse

The Gauchos of Southern Brazil are the inspiration for Grimpas's style of service, the "Rodizio." Moving about between the tables with their large sword-like skewers they will offer you a taste of this delicious memory of the Pampas.

8 passion fruits
1 tbsp. white sugar
1 (14-oz.) can sweetened condensed milk
2 C. heavy cream

1. Break passion fruits in half and scoop the pulp into a bowl. Use a little water to help rinse the juice out of the skins. Mix by hand to soften the pulp. Strain through a fine sieve or cheesecloth.

2. Stir in sugar and sweetened condensed milk.

3. In a chilled bowl, beat the heavy cream until stiff peaks form. Fold 1/3 of the cream into the passion fruit mixture, then quickly fold in the remaining cream until no streaks remain.

4. Chill for 1 hour and serve.

Signature Taste of MIAMI

Grimpa Steakhouse
901 Brickell Plaza, Miami, FL

"Life is too short for self-hatred and celery sticks."
Marilyn Wann

Crab and Sweet Corn Soup

Signature Tastes of MIAMI

4 cobs sweet corn
2 tbsp. peanut oil
½ C. finely diced white onion
2 tbsp. ginger, julienned
1 garlic clove finely diced
1 tsp. sea salt
½ C. shao hsing wine
7 C. Chinese chicken stock
½ lb. fresh crabmeat
1½ tsp. light soy sauce
2 eggs, lightly beaten
1 tbsp. green onion, finely sliced
ground white pepper

1. Remove kernels from corn cobs by running a sharp knife down the sides of each cob (yield: about 3 cups of corn kernels.)

2. Heat oil in a heavy-based pot and sauté onions, ginger, garlic and salt for 5 minutes.

3. Add wine and simmer until it has reduced by half.

4. Stir in corn and stock, bring to a boil and simmer gently for 30 minutes; skim occasionally during cooking.

5. Stir in the crabmeat and soy sauce, then lower heat and slowly pour the beaten eggs into the soup in a thin stream, stirring constantly with a fork. Remove soup from the heat as soon as you see the eggs forming fine "ribbons."

6. Serve the soup in bowls, garnished with green onions and ground white pepper.

4441 Collins Avenue, Miami Beach, FL

Hakkasan

"Two words to improve any dish. Ba, Con"
Ted Allen, The Iron Chef

Margherita Pizza

Harry's Pizzeria is our third restaurant, named after chef Michael Schwartz's son Harrison. From seasonally-inspired pizzas from the wood-burning oven to a new, welcoming counter where local and craft beers freely flow, Harry's radiates the relaxed, unpretentious vibe on which Michael's Genuine has built its reputation. More fun for us, and more fun for everybody, including our favorite local suppliers.

1 recipe prepared pizza dough, rolled to form a 12-inch thin-crust pie
1 tbsp. extra virgin olive oil
2 garlic cloves, finely chopped
3-4 large basil leaves, cut into strips
2 small tomatoes, thinly sliced
4 oz. mozzarella cheese, shredded
2 tbsp. parmesan cheese
Kosher salt and ground black pepper, to taste
crushed red pepper flakes, to taste

1. Preheat oven to 450°F.

2. Drizzle the olive oil over the pizza dough. Brush oil over entire surface including the crust.

3. Spread the finely chopped garlic evenly over the oiled crust. Sprinkle the mozzarella cheese over top, then place the thinly sliced tomatoes on top of the cheese. Lightly salt and pepper the tomatoes.Top with the fresh basil.

4. Bake the pizza in the oven for about 9-10 minutes, or until crust is crisp and cheese is melted and bubbling.

5. Add a little parmesan cheese and crushed red pepper, if desired and enjoy!

"For the first time I know what it is to eat. I have gained four pounds. I get frantically hungry, and the food I eat gives me a lingering pleasure. I never ate before in this deep carnal way... I want to bite into life and to be torn by it."
Anaïs Nin

Pan Con Bistec

A new restaurant in the heart of South Beach, which combines the flavors of traditional Cuban cuisine with the enchantment and sophistication of Havana in the 1950's. With elegant art deco touches, the interior décor of Havana 1957 embodies the jet set lifestyle of the movie stars that made Havana their playground. One of the most outstanding features of the restaurant is the classic Cuban Rum bar, which stocks over 70 varieties of rum from around the world.

2 tbsp. unsalted butter 2 tbsp. olive oil 1 large white onion, cut in half and sliced 1 (24-inch) loaf of Cuban bread (or baguette), sliced for sandwiches 1 lb. boneless rib-eye steak, sliced into ½-inch strips salt and pepper, to taste 1 tsp. dried parsley flakes 6 slices Swiss cheese, optional	**1.** In a large skillet, heat the butter and olive oil together and sauté the onion until slightly soft. Season with salt, remove the cooked onions from the skillet and set aside. **2.** In the same skillet, over high heat, sear the steak strips until brown, about 1 minute per side. Season with salt, pepper, and parsley flakes and remove steak from heat. **3.** Divide steak among sliced bread and cover the steak with onions and a slice of Swiss cheese, if desired. **4.** Preheat a panini sandwich press. **5.** Spread a thin layer of butter on the outside of each sandwich and press in a sandwich press until bread is toasted and cheese is melted.

405 Española Way, Miami Beach, FL

Havana

"As I ate the oysters with their strong taste of the sea and their faint metallic taste that the cold white wine washed away, leaving only the sea taste and the succulent texture, and as I drank their cold liquid from each shell and washed it down with the crisp taste of the wine, I lost the empty feeling and began to be happy, and to make plans."
Ernest Hemingway

Chicken Saltimbocca

Hosteria Romana originated its activities in 2001 on the harmonized street, Española Way, in the heart of South Beach. From the beginning, Hosteria Romana has pleased and satisfied the exigencies of hundreds of thousands of customers both tourists and locals alike. Only at Hosteria Romana will patrons truly feel the ambience of Italy itself and enjoy exceptional Italian delicacies like our Bucatini alla Amatriciana, Agnolotti fatti a casa, Carbonara alla romana, and Carciofi alla Giudia. Also enjoy the fresh fish and live lobster or our very own Filet Mignon dishes.

8 chicken breasts
3 tbsp. sweet butter, melted
5 large sage leaves, fresh or preserved in salt
1 tsp. rosemary leaves, fresh, preserved in salt or dried and blanched
1 tsp. dried marjoram
1 tsp. salt
¼ tsp. freshly ground black pepper
1 tbsp. olive oil
8 slices prosciutto di Parma

1. Finely chop the sage, rosemary and marjoram and place in a bowl. Add the melted butter, salt and pepper, and mix well.

2. Cut a large sheet of aluminum foil and brush the shiny side with olive oil.

3. Using a pastry brush, coat each piece of chicken with the herb-butter mixture. Wrap each piece in a slice of prosciutto di Parma, then place the chicken pieces on the foil close together and wrap completely with foil.

4. Place the package in a terra cotta or ceramic casserole dish and cover. Place the casserole in a cold oven and turn the oven temperature to 450°F.

5. Bake, covered, for 1 hour and 45 minutes. Remove from oven and let stand for 5 minutes. Use scissors to cut from the center of the foil outward in four directions, making a cross.

6. Cut each quarter in half and fold back each of the foil pieces from the center, forming petals over each side of the casserole dish. Serve immediately.

Hosteria Romana
429 Espanola Way Miami, FL

"The greatest delight the fields and woods minister is the suggestion of an occult relation between man and the vegetable. I am not alone and unacknowledged. They nod to me and I to them."
Ralph Waldo Emerson

Thit Kho

Hy Vong, which means "hope" in Vietnamese, offers a remarkable culinary experience to food lovers in the form of simple, delicious meals in an intimate, relaxed environment. We pride ourselves on using only the freshest ingredients and preparing each dish with the highest level of care and attention. Our fish is brought in by local fishermen daily, our fruits and vegetables are hand selected, and our rice paper is home-made. We look forward to making you a meal at a home away from home.

1 lb. pork (choose the belly or parts with medium level of fat)
1 coconut (or ½ can of coconut juice plus 2 C. unsweetened dried coconut flakes)
3 tbsp. fish sauce
2 tbsp. sugar
1 tbsp. molasses
salt and pepper, to taste

1. To remove the coconut meat from the shell, pierce one or more of the eyes with an ice pick. Drain the coconut liquid though a fine-mesh sieve and reserve. Place the coconut in a 350°F oven for 15-20 minutes; remove from the oven. Firmly tap the coconut with a hammer to crack open the shell. Continue tapping the shell until it is cracked in several places. Remove as much of the shell as possible this way. Remove the meat by inserting a sharp knife between the meat and shell or score the flesh and lift from the edge. Remove the brown tissue adhering to the meat prior to grating to maintain a snow-white color. Remove the tissue with a knife or vegetable peeler while still warm. Cut coconut meat into long pieces.

2. Slice pork into thin pieces, mix with fish sauce, sugar, molasses and let marinate for 20 minutes.

3. Place pork into a saucepan and braise over low heat until it shrinks a little and absorb the spices.

4. Put coconut liquid and coconut meat (or shredded coconut) into the pan with the pork and cook until liquid thickens.

5. Serve the pork over hot steamed rice with vegetables.

3458 Southwest 8th Street, Miami, FL

Hy-Vong

"He who distinguishes the true savor of his food can never be a glutton; he who does not cannot be otherwise."
Henry David Thoreau

Brooklyn Style Pizza

I Love Pizza uses organic flour to create its thin-crust, toasted-to-perfection dough and tops it with a delectable sauce prepared daily with garden-fresh tomatoes. Our great variety of toppings will certainly satisfy meat lovers and vegetarians alike. Try one of our signature pies—the Brooklyn, the Uptown, the Five Points or simply create your own pizza by choosing from our extensive selection of toppings. And for the chocolate lover ... don't forget to order our luscious Nutella Pizza.

1 tsp. active dry yeast
¼ C. warm water
1 C. cold water
1 tsp. salt
3 C. bread flour
6 oz. low-moisture mozzarella cheese, thinly sliced
4 oz. canned crushed tomatoes
¼ tsp. freshly-ground black pepper
½ tsp. dried oregano
3 tbsp. extra virgin olive oil
6 leaves fresh basil, torn

1. Sprinkle yeast over warm water in a large bowl. Let stand for 5 minutes to proof. Stir in salt and cold water, then stir in the flour about 1 cup at a time. When the dough comes together, remove from the bowl, knead on a floured surface until smooth, about 10 minutes.

2. Divide into two pieces, and form each one into a tight ball. Coat the dough balls with olive oil, and refrigerate in a sealed container for at least 16 hours. Be sure to use a big enough container to allow the dough to rise. Remove the dough from the refrigerator one hour prior to using.

3. Preheat the oven, with a pizza stone on the lowest rack, to 500°F. Lightly dust a pizza peel with flour.

4. Using one ball of dough at a time, lightly dust the dough with flour, and stretch gradually until it is about 14 inches in diameter. Place on the floured peel.

5. Place thin slices of mozzarella over the dough, then grind a liberal amount of black pepper on top. Sprinkle with dried oregano. Arrange crushed tomatoes and basil over top, leaving some empty areas. Drizzle with olive oil.

6. Place pizza on pizza stone, turn down oven to 450°F, and bake for 12-14 minutes or until crust is browned and cheese is melted and bubbly.

7105 Collins Avenue Miami Beach, FL

I Love Pizza

"Tell me what you eat, I'll tell you who you are."
Anthelme Brillat-Savarin

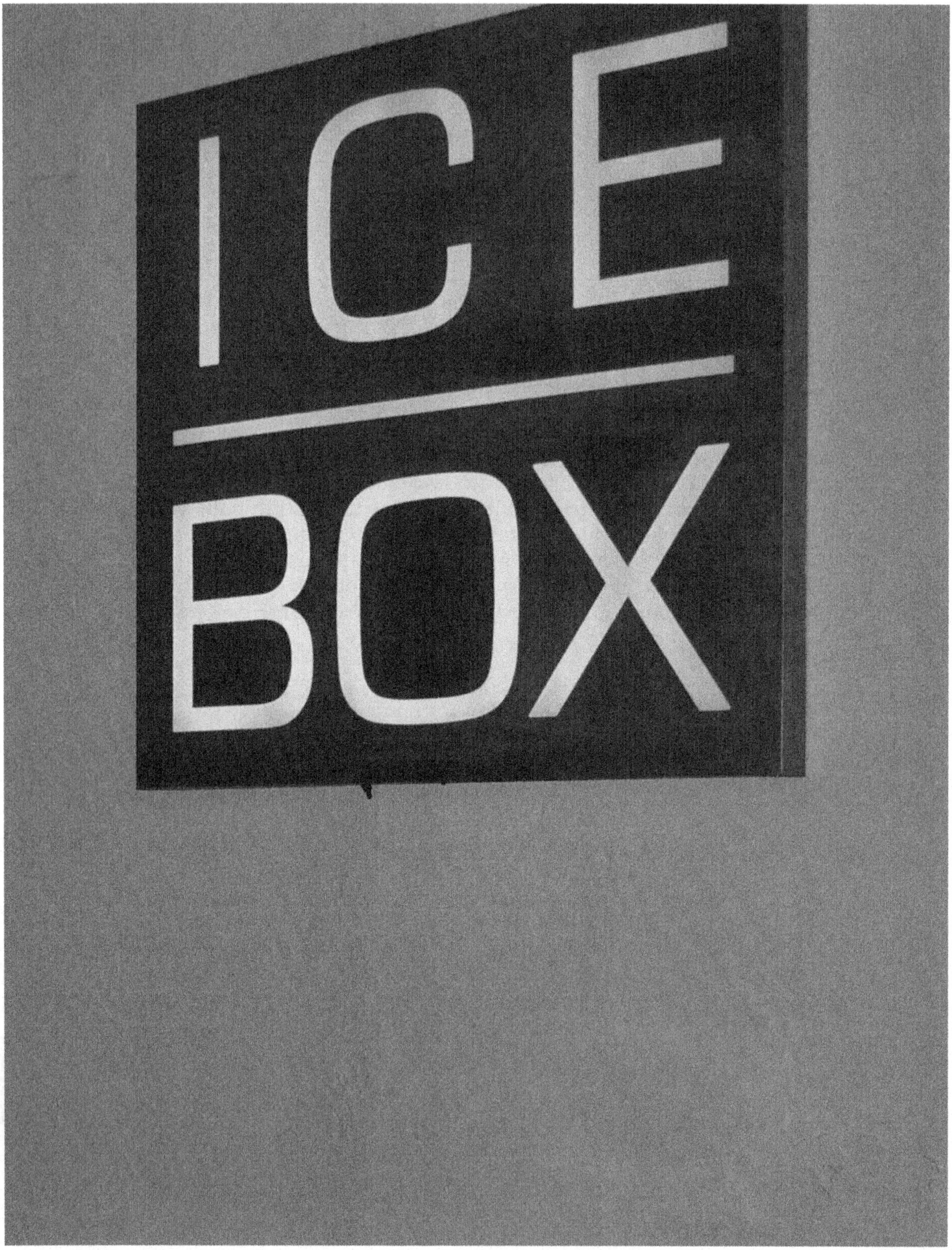
ICE
BOX

Brisket Sandwich

Signature Tastes of MIAMI

The Icebox Way is more than just food; it is a lifestyle that celebrates variety and quality. Plus, it's about community. Icebox is constantly looking for ways to remain relevant to the community; to remain within it Icebox is constantly evolving and changing with the needs and tastes of the community. Lastly, and most notably, we are constantly reinventing our menu to keep things fresh and prevent our customers from tiring of our menu.

Rub:
¼ C. paprika
¼ C. freshly-ground black pepper
⅛ C. salt
¼ C. brown sugar
2 tbsp. chili powder
¼ C. garlic powder
1 (10-lb.) beef brisket

Braise Mix:
7 slices bacon, cut in 1-inch pieces
3 yellow onions, julienned
3 tomatoes, sliced
2 ribs celery, halved
3 jalapeños
1 red pepper, seeded and julienned
3 carrots, julienned
12 oz. oatmeal stout
¼ C. cider vinegar
2 tbsp. Worcestershire sauce
handful garlic, abt. 12 cloves
whole-wheat buns
sliced red onion and pickles, for serving

Brisket BBQ Sauce:
olive oil
4 shallots, diced
1 (No.10) can diced tomatoes
1 (64-oz.) can sliced peaches
16 oz. dried figs, stems removed
1 stem rosemary, leaves picked
½ C. balsamic vinegar
¼ C. stone-ground mustard
1 lemon, juiced
⅓ C. packed grated fresh ginger
4 C. fresh orange juice
2 C. white tequila (reposado)
1 tbsp. dry mustard
8 ancho chiles
1 tbsp. sambal oelek
2 tsp. salt
1 C. brown sugar
1 can anchovies, minced
10 cloves garlic, peeled

1. Mix all of the dry rub ingredients together in a small bowl. Dry brisket with paper towels. Coat the brisket all over with the dry rub.

2. Make a mesquite fire inside the oven of a smoker. A combination of charcoal and mesquite chips (wet) is fine. Put the brisket on the right side of the grates in the main oven of the smoker. Damp down the fire. Leave the brisket to smoke until the fire burns out.

3. Meanwhile, in a large skillet, sauté the bacon and vegetables until they are moist. Transfer to a 6-inch deep, full-sized hotel pan or roasting pan. Add the brisket, beer, vinegar, Worcestershire and garlic. Cover the pan with a sheet of parchment paper and tightly cover with a sheet of heavy foil. Cook 8 hours in a 250°F oven. Reserve pan juices for bbq sauce.

4. Cut the brisket into chunks and serve on whole-wheat buns with the bbq sauce, sliced red onion, and pickles.

Brisket BBQ Sauce:

1. Heat about ¼ cup of oil in a heavy-bottomed pan over medium heat. Add the shallots and sauté for a couple of minutes. Add the remaining ingredients and bring to slow boil—be careful not to burn. Cook on ultra-low heat for about 8 hours. Cool.

2. Add the sauce to a food processor and blend to combine. Dilute with reserved brisket pan juices before serving.

1657 Michigan Avenue, Miami, FL

Icebox Cafe

"I went to a restaurant that serves 'breakfast at any time'. So I ordered French Toast during the Renaissance."
Steven Wright

Insalata Mista

Italian with a vaunted pedigree: The founders of Il Mulino left New York to open Miami's Il Gabbiano, which now regularly shows up near the top of many Best Restaurants in Florida lists. Feast on calvados-braised chicken breast, fettucini alfredo, and no less than a dozen veal dishes. Yes, you'll have the tiramisu.

⅓ C. lightly packed fresh basil leaves
⅓ C. white wine vinegar or fresh lemon juice
1 tsp. salt, plus more for seasoning
½ tsp. freshly ground black pepper, plus more for seasoning
½ C. extra virgin olive oil
8 C. arugula
4 C. bite-size pieces radicchio, from 1 (10-oz.) head
1 carrot, peeled
1 hothouse cucumber, peeled

1. Blend the basil, vinegar, 1 teaspoon of salt, and ½ teaspoon of pepper in a blender. With the machine running, gradually blend in the oil.

2. Place the arugula and radicchio in a wide shallow bowl.

3. Using a vegetable peeler, shave the carrot over the salad.

4. Shave the cucumber into a medium bowl. Pat the cucumber shavings with paper towels to absorb the excess moisture. Add the cucumbers to the salad.

5. Toss the salad with enough dressing to coat. Season the salad, to taste, with salt and pepper, and serve.

335 South Biscayne Boulevard, Miami, FL

Il Gabbiano

"You can never have enough garlic. With enough garlic, you can eat the *New York Times.*"
Morley Safer

Tortilla de Papa y Cebolla

Islas Canarias Restaurant is a family restaurant that was established in 1977 by Raul and Amelia Garcia and their two children Nancy and Santiago. Raul's family recipes have been preserved throughout the years under the careful watch of his children. During the humble beginnings, Raul and Amelia catered to the people of Miami, and many of their first customers have over the years become pillars of our community. Today, our core customers consist of the children of those families for whom Raul prepared special meals.

½ C. extra virgin olive oil
2 garlic cloves, mashed
4 large potatoes, peeled and cut in ⅛-inch half moons
1 large Spanish onion, thinly sliced in half moons
6 large eggs
salt and pepper

1. Heat oil in 9-inch omelette pan. Fry garlic until golden and discard. Add potato slices and cook over medium heat. Add onions after 5 minutes; cook until potatoes are tender. Turn potatoes and onions as they cook.

2. In a large bowl, beat eggs with a fork or wire whisk until slightly foamy; add salt and pepper to taste.

3. With a slotted spoon, drain potatoes and onions and add to the eggs. Return egg and potato mixture to same skillet, adding more oil if necessary so that eggs do not stick. Spread evenly and cook over medium heat, shaking the pan occasionally.

4. When eggs leave sides of pan, invert a plate over the pan and flip omelette onto plate. Slide omelette back into pan to brown other side.

5. Serve hot or at room temperature on a round china or glass plate.

13695 Southwest 26th Street, Miami, FL

Islas Canarias

"Enchant, stay beautiful and graceful, but do this, eat well. Bring the same consideration to the preparation of your food as you devote to your appearance. Let your dinner be a poem, like your dress."
Charles Pierre Monselet, French journalist

Massaman Curry

Peter Hongnopkhun has been a successful restauranteur for over 20 years in the Margate area. His authentic approach to Thai dining allows for a unique cultural experience. Together with his son Ben and daughter Christine, Peter has built a family-friendly restaurant with a comfortable atmosphere and affordable dishes. Jasmine Thai and Sushi has been a proud member of the Margate restaurant community for 20 years. Rated and reviewed in the Zagat Survey and praised frequently by local papers such as the Sun Sentinel and the Miami Herald, Jasmine Thai and Peter Hongnopkhun deliver a perfect night out.

Curry Paste:
10 dried chilies, roasted, soaked and seeded
½ tsp. black peppercorns, roasted
1 tsp. coriander seeds, roasted
1 tsp. cumin seeds, roasted
2 cloves, roasted
2 cardamom pods, roasted
1 tsp. shrimp paste, wrapped in tin foil, roasted
½ tsp. ground nutmeg
1 tsp. salt
1 tsp. magroot skin
1 tsp. galangal
1 tsp. coriander roots
1 tbsp. lemongrass
¼ C. shallots
2 tbsp. garlic

4 tbsp. curry paste
3 tbsp. vegetable oil
2 lbs. chicken legs and thighs
1 C. coconut cream plus 1 C. coconut milk
1 C. white potatoes
1 C. onions, or peeled whole shallots
4 cardamom pods
¼ C. roasted peanuts, whole
1 tbsp. palm sugar
1-inch piece of cinnamon stick
2 dried cassia leaves
2 tbsp. fish sauce
2 tbsp. tamarind paste

1. Dry roast the dry spices for the curry paste in a pan over medium heat until fragrant, about 2-4 minutes. Roast the shrimp paste wrapped in tin foil for a few minutes. Brown the chilies.

2. Grind the dried spices until powdered, set aside.

3. Grind the chilies in a food processor, then add the rest of the ingredients, the dried spice powder, and the shrimp paste. Blend well.

4. Cut the potatoes and onions into bite-sized pieces and wash the chicken.

5. Add the oil to the pan and turn to medium high. Fry 4 tablespoons of the paste until fragrant, about 3-4 minutes. Keep stirring so it doesn't burn.

6. Add the whole chicken pieces. Fry until the chicken is seared on the outside, about 2-3 minutes.

7. Add 1 cup of the coconut cream (top part of the can if using canned—don't shake the can). Simmer until the oil separates, about 2-3 minutes.

8. Add the potatoes, peanuts and onions and the 1 cup of coconut milk. Simmer for a few minutes.

9. Add the cinnamon, cardamom seeds, cassia leaves.

10. Simmer (and stir well) until the mixture browns and oil comes to the top. About 15-20 minutes. If it gets too dry, add some water. Add the fish sauce, palm sugar and tamarind juice at the end.

11. Serve with rice, roti or ajaat (pickled cucumber salad).

Grilled Mahi Mahi

Jimmy'z Kitchen cuisine and menu is a large variety of Panini, sandwiches, large salads and Daily Chef Specials. We take pride in using only the freshest and highest quality products prepared to order by our trained chefs. We are a proven counter-service, take-out, delivery and catering restaurant of fine, healthy, food of the highest quality.

4 (8-oz.) mahi mahi fillets
2 tbsp. olive oil
2 tbsp. fresh ginger, minced
1 tbsp. garlic, minced
1 tbsp. fresh lime juice
¼ C. soy sauce
2 tbsp. honey
2 tbsp. dry red wine
⅛ tbsp. cayenne pepper (or to taste)
salt and pepper

1. In a bowl, mix together all ingredients except the mahi mahi. Pour marinade into a 1 gallon zipper bag, add mahi mahi and seal; refrigerate at least 4 hours or overnight.

2. Spray a grill pan with non-stick cooking spray and heat over medium to medium-high heat.

3. Grill mahi mahi on hot grill pan for 6 minutes per side for a 1-inch fillet or until fish is firm and opaque.

Jimmy'z Kitchen
2700 North Miami Avenue Miami, FL

"Grilling, broiling, barbecuing—whatever you want to call it—is an art, not just a matter of building a pyre and throwing on a piece of meat as a sacrifice to the gods of the stomach."
James Beard

In 1913, Joe Weiss opened up a small lunch counter on Miami Beach. Back then, Miami Beach was just a quiet, backwater town. Folks stopped in to chat and for a top-notch fish sandwich and fries. This, of course, was only the beginning, and what happened next is a story worth telling.

1 lb. jumbo lump crabmeat, picked over
½ red bell pepper, chopped
¼ C. chopped onion
4 scallions, trimmed and chopped
¼ C. chopped fresh parsley
1 garlic clove, minced
1 egg, lightly beaten
2 tbsp. Dijon mustard
2 tbsp. fresh lemon juice
½ tsp. Worcestershire sauce
¼ tbsp. Tabasco sauce
¾ C. fine dry bread crumbs
2 tbsp. vegetable oil, plus more if needed
lime or lemon wedges, for garnish
salsa, for serving

1. In a large mixing bowl, combine the crabmeat, red pepper, onion, scallions, parsley, and garlic.

2. In a small bowl, stir together the egg, mustard, lemon juice, Worcestershire, and Tabasco.

3. Gently fold this mixture into the crabmeat mixture; then add ¼ cup of the bread crumbs, mixing gently just until combined.

4. Form 8 (½-inch thick patties), using ½ cup of the crabmeat mixture for each. Coat the patties with the remaining bread crumbs and place them on a wax paper-lined baking sheet. Refrigerate until set, at least 1 hour.

5. Heat the oil in a large skillet over medium heat. Add 4 of the crab cakes at a time. Cook until golden, about 5 minutes, then gently flip and cook until golden on the other side.

6. Serve hot, garnished with lime or lemon wedges, or with a small cup of salsa on the side, if desired.

Joe's Stone Crab
11 Washington Avenue Miami Beach, FL

"All sorrows are less with bread."
Miguel de Cervantes, Don Quixote

Ceviche

Juvia is a 10,000 square foot indoor/outdoor restaurant and lounge on the penthouse level of the parking garage by Herzog & de Meuron at 1111 Lincoln Road. Owned and operated by Jonas and Alexandra Millan of Bonito St. Barth, Juvia's dining room features a vertical garden, designed by internationally acclaimed botanist Patrick Blanc, which invokes the lushness of the Amazon rainforest.

7 oz. octopus, cooked, cut into bite-size pieces
7 oz. shrimp, blanched
7 oz. sea scallops, cooked, cut into small pieces if large
1 red onion, diced very fine
½ red aji limo chile, minced
½ yellow aji limo chile, minced
16 key limes, juiced
salt
2 sweet potatoes, boiled (of the camote variety, if you can find them)
1 large fresh ear corn on the cob, cooked and cut into rounds (choclo variety, if you can find them)

1. Mix seafood with the minced onion in large bowl.

2. Season seafood mixture with salt and aji limo chiles.

3. Toss seafood in the lime juice. Chill with ice cubes, mixing well. Remove ice before it melts.

4. Serve on bed of lettuce with sweet potato and boiled corn rounds.

1111 Lincoln Road Miami Beach, FL

Juvia

"There are people who strictly deprive themselves of each and every eatable, drinkable, and smokable which has in any way acquired a shady reputation. They pay this price for health. And health is all they get for it. How strange it is. It is like paying out your whole fortune for a cow that has gone dry."
Mark Twain

Tuna Tartare

Since 1998 Kam Wah has been providing the Kendall area with exquisite Thai, Chinese, and Japanese dishes. It is a family-owned restaurant that places emphasis on quality and customer satisfaction. Many have claimed that our taste is unmatched. Come in and see for yourself! We promise you'll enjoy our unique flavors.

Signature Tastes of MIAMI

3¾ lbs. very fresh tuna steak
1¼ C. olive oil
5 limes, zest grated
1 C. freshly squeezed lime juice
2½ tsp. wasabi powder
2½ tbsp. soy sauce
2 tbsp. red pepper sauce
2½ tbsp. Kosher salt
1½ tbsp. freshly ground black pepper
1¼ C. minced scallions, white and green parts (approx. 12 scallions)
3¼ tbsp. minced fresh jalapeño pepper, seeds removed
5 ripe Hass avocados
1½ tbsp. toasted sesame seeds, optional

1. Cut the tuna into ¼-inch dice and place it in a very large bowl.

2. In a separate bowl, combine the olive oil, lime zest, lime juice, wasabi, soy sauce, red pepper sauce, salt, and pepper.

3. Pour mixture over the tuna, add the scallions and jalapeño, and mix well.

4. Cut the avocados in half, remove the seed, and peel. Cut the avocados into ¼-inch dice. Carefully mix the avocado into the tuna mixture.

5. Add the toasted sesame seeds, if using, and season to taste.

6. Allow the mixture to sit in the refrigerator for at least 1 hour for the flavors to blend. Serve with crisp crackers.

Kam Wah Restaurant
12895 Southwest 42nd Street, Miami, FL

"All you need is love. But a little chocolate now and then doesn't hurt."
Charles M. Schulz

los mejores pasteles de Miami

Karla BAKERY

Principal · Menu · Contactenos

Bienvenido a Karla Bakery,

Convenientemente localizado en el corazon de Miami nuestro deseo es proveer a nuestros clientes con buen servicio y dulces de alta calidad. Ofrecemos una gran variedad de postres, panes, cakes y los deliciosos pastelitos cubanos entre otros para alagar su paladar de dulces tradicionales. Nuestras recetas han sido pasadas de generacion a generacion de panaderos cubanos y se han mantenido lo mas originales para asegurar la mejor calidad.

Welcome to Karla Bakery,

Conveniently located in the heart of Miami our goal is to provide our clients with quality sweets and good service. We have a variety of desserts, breads, cakes and the delicious Cuban pastelitos among others to fulfill your desire of traditional sweet. Our recipes have been passed down from generations of Cuban bakers and are kept as true as possible to their original to ensure the best quality pastries.

Chicken Cordon Bleu

Signature Tastes of MIAMI

4 skinless, boneless chicken breast halves
¼ tsp. salt
⅛ tsp. ground black pepper
6 slices Swiss cheese
4 slices cooked ham
½ C. seasoned bread crumbs

1. Preheat oven to 350°F. Coat a 9x13-inch baking dish with non-stick cooking spray.

2. Pound chicken breasts to ¼-inch thickness.

3. Sprinkle each piece of chicken on both sides with salt and pepper. Place 1 cheese slice and 1 ham slice on top of each breast. Roll up each breast and secure with a toothpick. Place in baking dish and sprinkle chicken evenly with bread crumbs.

4. Bake for 30 to 35 minutes, or until chicken is no longer pink.

5. Remove from oven, and place ½ cheese slice on top of each breast. Return to oven for 3 to 5 minutes, or until cheese has melted. Remove toothpicks, and serve immediately.

Karla Bakery

6474 West Flagler Street, Miami, FL

Huevos Fritos (Fried Fish Roe)

In 1976, the brothers decided to equip their fish market with deep fryers and u-shaped counters so that they could serve their daily catch. "Los Paraditos", so nick-named by La Camaronera has been a Cuban fish-fry at its best from the very start.

300 g. fish roe, whole, rinsed, (if smaller than 3 inches left whole, cut into small pieces if large)
½ tsp. turmeric
1 tbsp. chili paste
salt, to taste
oil, for frying

1. In a dish, mix the chili powder, turmeric, and salt together until a paste forms.

2. Put the roe into the paste, turn to coat, and marinate for 1 hour.

3. In a large frying pan, shallow fry the roe in oil over medium heat, turning occasionally. Cover the frying pan as the roe may "pop" in hot oil.

4. Drain and serve with fries and your favorite sauce.

La Camaronera Seafood Joint and Fish Market
1952 W Flagler St Miami, FL

"I love you like a fat kid loves cake!"
Scott Adams

La Gelateria started under Gelateria Parmalat in 1996. We opened our first store in Atlanta and then our second and most successful store in South Beach Florida on the world renowned Lincoln Road on January 6, 2000. After the fall of Parmalat in 2003 the Nasser Family acquired all the stores in the US and changed the name to La Gelateria. Since then we have won numerous awards from Entertainment Weekly, The Travel and Discovery Channel and The Food Network, to name a few. Since the first day that we opened our doors our motto has never changed... "The BEST gelato you will ever taste." Being a family business we are adamant about quality and service above all.

6 oz. bittersweet chocolate, chopped
2 oz. semisweet chocolate, chopped
10 tbsp. (1¼ sticks) unsalted butter
½ C. all-purpose flour
1½ C. confectioners' sugar, sifted
3 large eggs
3 egg yolks
1 tsp. vanilla extract
2 tbsp. orange liqueur

1. Preheat oven to 425°F.

2. Grease 6 (6-oz.) ramekins and set aside.

3. Melt the chocolates and butter together in the microwave, or in a double boiler until smooth. Pour into a large mixing bowl.

4. Add the flour and sugar to chocolate mixture and stir until just blended.

5. Stir in the eggs and yolks and mix until smooth.

6. Stir in the vanilla and orange liqueur.

7. Divide the batter evenly among the ramekins and place in the oven and bake for 14 minutes. The edges will be firm but the center should be molten.

8. Run a knife around the edges to loosen and invert gateaux onto dessert plates. Serve with vanilla gelato or dust with confectioners' sugar.

La Gelateria
670 Lincoln Road, Miami Beach, FL

"Ask not what you can do for your country. Ask what's for lunch."
Orson Welles

Fried Fish Sandwich

Signature Tastes of MIAMI

In 1993 we opened our first restaurant in Aruba Island, with the idea of making the Peruvian-style rotisserie chicken and some Peruvian plates known on the Island. The idea worked great, and our food was not only known but it became part of the Arubian daily meal. Because of this success, we decided to introduce the same idea in Florida, so in 1995 we opened our first location here, in Margate. The results were even better.

2 lb. grouper, mahi mahi, cod, or halibut fillets
2 tsp. Greek seasoning, divided
1½ tsp. salt, divided
1 tsp. freshly ground pepper, divided
2¼ C. all-purpose flour
¼ C. yellow cornmeal
2 tsp. baking powder
2 C. cold beer
1 large egg, lightly beaten
vegetable oil
4 hamburger buns, split
tartar sauce or mayonnaise
4 green leaf lettuce leaves
4 tomato slices

1. Cut fish into 3-inch strips. Sprinkle evenly with 1 tsp. Greek seasoning, 1 tsp. salt, and ½ tsp. pepper.

2. Combine flour, cornmeal, baking powder, remaining 1 tsp. Greek seasoning, ½ tsp. salt, and ½ tsp. pepper; stir well. Add 2 cups cold beer and egg, stirring until thoroughly blended and smooth.

3. Pour oil to a depth of 2 to 3 inches in a Dutch oven; heat to 375°F.

4. Dip fish strips into batter, coating both sides well; shake off excess. Fry fish, in batches, 2 minutes on each side or until golden (do not crowd pan). Drain on paper towels.

5. Spread top half of each bun evenly with tartar sauce. Place 1 lettuce leaf and 1 tomato slice on bottom half of each bun; top each with 2 fried fish strips and top halves of buns.

127 Southeast 2nd Avenue, Miami, FL

La Granja

"If more of us valued food and cheer above hoarded gold, it would be a much merrier world."
J.R.R. Tolkien

LA LICUADORA

PERUVIAN FOOD

WE DELIVERY

PH: 305-379-0000

COMBO # 1
1/4 CHICKEN WITH 2 SIDE ORDERS
1/4 pollo con 2 acomponentes
$ 5.99

COMBO # 2
1/2 CHICKEN WITH 2 SIDE ORDERS
1/2 pollo con 2 acompanantes
$ 9.99

COMBO # 3
1 CHICKEN WITH 2 SIDE ORDERS
1 pollo con 2 acompanantes
$ 16.99

COMBO # 4
1 CHICKEN WITH 2 SIDE ORDERS AND 2LTRS SODA

Peruvian Style Rotisserie Chicken

POLLOS A LA BRASA AL ESTILO PERUANO

NOW IN DOWNTOWN MIAMI!!!
Dine-in * Take Out * Delivery
OPEN LATE!!!
La Licuadora

Design your own combo

1/4 CHICKEN (Dark Meat) $3.99
1/4 de Pollo a la Brasa (Pecho)
1/4 CHICKEN (White Meat) $4.50
1/4 de Pollo a la Brasa (Pierna)
1/2 CHICKEN $7.50
1/2 Pollo a la Brasa
WHOLE CHICKEN $13.99
Pollo Entero

Order on line at

www.licuadorarestaurant.com

SIDE ORDERS	MED	LARGE
White Rice	$1.99	$2.50

Mojarra Frita

At La Licuadora, we keep the rich heritage of Peruvian cuisine alive by preparing only the best and most authentic Peruvian inspired dishes. We offer a full menu including breakfast fare (try our perfectly seasoned Huevos Fritos!) as well as the opportunity to select your own favorite dishes and create your own combo. We've been told our Papas Fritas are the best in Miami!

2 (10-oz.) whole, fresh tilapia, cleaned and scaled
6-8 cloves garlic, mashed to a paste
3 limes, juiced
1 tsp. salt, or to taste
1 tsp. ground black pepper
1 large or 2 small tomatoes, diced
½ onion, minced
1 serrano chili pepper or jalapeño, minced
½ C. cilantro, minced

1. With a sharp knife, make several angled slits along the body of the fish, cutting down to the rib bones. Make two lateral slits along the back of the fish, from head to tail, on either side of the dorsal fin. These cuts will ensure quick cooking and maximum crispiness.

2. Mix garlic, lime juice, salt and pepper together. Rub all over the fish and stuff into the slits.

3. Heat a generous amount of olive oil in a frying pan over medium-high heat. Add fish and pan-fry until browned on both sides, about 3 minutes per side. Set aside, loosely cover with foil.

4. In the same pan, sauté the onions and pepper until onion is translucent and fragrant.

5. Add the diced tomato and cilantro and season with a little salt.

6. Add fish back to the pan and cover. Steam for about 5-10 minutes until tomatoes release some of their juices. Serve fish with pan juices.

La Licuadora

47 Northeast 2nd Avenue, Miami, FL

"Popcorn for breakfast! Why not? It's a grain. It's like, like, grits, but with high self-esteem."
James Patterson, The Angel Experiment

Zuppa del Giorno

Hailed by Zagat for its excellent service and delectable home-made cuisine, La Locanda reinvents itself relocating to a renovated space, boasting a sleek, stylish interior with ceiling-high stone walls, dark wood, white linen table-tops, fresh flowers, and candlelight, creating the ultimate cool, intimate ambiance to indulge in sumptuous Italian cuisine while enjoying a great selection of wines and a full service bar. LCD Flat screens will entice loyal "Heat" fans for prime-time game watching.

2¾ C. chicken stock or broth
¼ C. heavy cream
3 medium russet potatoes
2 C. chopped kale
½ lb. spicy Italian sausage
¼ tsp. salt
¼ tsp. crushed red pepper flake

1. Place the stock pot on the stove burner. Set the burner to medium-low heat using the dial located on the stove's control panel.
2. Open the chicken stock, with a can opener if needed, and measure the prescribed amount using measuring cups. Pour the measured stock into the stock pot.
3. Fold open the heavy cream container and measure the appropriate amount using a measuring cup. Pour the measured amount of cream into the stock pot.
4. Open sausage package with knife. Remove the skin on the sausage. This is done by lightly slicing the sausage lengthwise and gently tugging at the skin bordering the cut.
5. Grill or sauté the sausage in the skillet on a separate stove burner set to medium heat. Use the spatula to flip the sausage so it does not burn.
6. When thoroughly cooked, remove the sausage from the skillet using a pair of tongs and place on a paper towel. Allow the sausage to cool.
7. Rinse the potatoes and kale in the sink to remove any dirt or residue.
8. Slice the unpeeled potato into quarters on the vegetable cutting board using a knife. Cut each quarter into ¼" slices. Add the potato slices to the stock pot.
9. Chop the kale into bite size pieces on the vegetable cutting board using a knife. Add the kale to the stock pot.
10. When cool enough to touch, place the sausage on the meat cutting board. Cut the sausage with a fresh knife. The sausage should be cut at an angle into slices about ½" thick.
11. Blot the pieces of sausage with paper towels. This decreases the amount of oil which goes into the soup.
12. Add the sausage to the stock pot.
13. Retract the metal tab on the salt and pour the amount mentioned above into a measuring spoon. Combine with the chicken stock in the stock pot.

La Locanda
419 Washington Avenue, Miami Beach, FL

"Seize the moment. Remember all those women on the *Titanic* who waved off the dessert cart."
Erma Bombeck

Strawberry Spinach Salad

Signature Tastes of MIAMI

Established in 2001 La Loggia is deemed one of the pioneers in the revitalization of Downtown Miami. Excellent reviews from Miami Herald and Zagat's. Known for its power lunches and popular Happy Hours!

¼ C. slivered almonds
2 tbsp. sugar
1 (10-oz.) package fresh spinach, torn
1 C. fresh strawberries, sliced

Dressing:
2 tbsp. canola oil
1 tbsp. raspberry vinegar
1 green onion, finely chopped
1½ tsp. sugar
1½ tsp. Worcestershire sauce
1 tsp. poppy seeds
¼ tsp. salt
dash of paprika

1. In a large skillet, cook and stir almonds and sugar over low heat until sugar is dissolved and almonds are coated. Spread on foil to cool; break apart.

2. In a large salad bowl, combine the spinach, strawberries and almonds.

3. In a jar with a tight-fitting lid, combine the dressing ingredients; shake well.

4. Drizzle over salad; toss gently to coat. Serve immediately.

La Loggia Ristorante
68 West Flagler Street
Miami, FL

"Writers fish for the right words like fishermen fish for, um, whatever those aquatic creatures with fins and gills are called."
Jarod Kintz

139

Chicken Cobb

This friendly Colombian joint, half neighborhood restaurant, half late night hangout, is the last stop for hungry Little Havana and Brickell Village clubgoers in need of sustenance at the end of a long night. It is open until 6 a.m. Thursday through Saturday, but its low prices and tasty, substantial food also attract young Latino families earlier in the evening and office workers at lunchtime.

2 (8-oz.) boneless, skinless chicken breasts
2 tsp. plus 2 tbsp. extra virgin olive oil
1 tsp. poultry seasoning
salt and freshly ground black pepper
4 large eggs
8 slices bacon, chopped into ½-inch pieces
3 hearts romaine lettuce
2 lemons, juiced
2 ripe avocados, halved and scooped from skins with a spoon, then diced
2 vine-ripened tomatoes, seeded and diced
1 red onion, chopped
2 C. white cheddar or Monterey Jack, shredded (or substitute blue cheese crumbled)

1. Heat a grill pan or non-stick skillet over medium-high heat. Coat chicken breasts with 2 teaspoons oil, poultry seasoning, salt and pepper.
2. Grill or pan-fry chicken 6 to 7 minutes on each side. Remove from heat and let rest 5 minutes. Halve chicken breasts and chop the meat.
3. In a small pot, cover eggs with cold water. Place over high heat and bring water to a boil. Once it comes to a boil, cover the pot and turn off the heat. Set a timer for 10 minutes. After the 10 minutes, cool eggs under cold running water. Peel and chop.
4. Cook chopped bacon in a skillet over medium-high heat until crisp. Drain on paper towels.
5. Chop hearts of romaine lettuce and place in a large serving platter or salad bowl. Dress chopped lettuce with the juice of 1½ lemons. Drizzle remaining 2 tablespoons extra-virgin olive oil over lettuce. Season greens with salt and pepper, to taste.
6. Toss diced avocados with juice of remaining ½ lemon, to stop from browning.
7. To serve, arrange rows of chopped chicken, chopped hard boiled egg, crisp bacon bits, diced avocado, diced tomato, chopped red onion and shredded cheese on top of either 4 individual portions of dressed romaine or 1 large serving platter.

97 Southwest 8th Street, Miami, FL

La Moon

"One cannot think well, love well, sleep well, if one has not dined well."
Virginia Woolf

Chicken Quesadillas

Signature Tastes of MIAMI

Elegance, indulgence, sophistication. Each is a virtue at La Riviera—the signature restaurant at Sofitel Miami—where French cuisine and Mediterranean flavors unite, with just a hint of Latin influence. Stylishly appointed, as a reflection of our chic South Florida address, this exquisite Miami French restaurant provides a treat not only for the palette, but from a visual perspective as well—with breathtaking views of the hotel's vibrant gardens and the sparkling Blue Lagoon beyond. Enjoy an extraordinarily sensory Miami French dining experience, where vivid red glasses and floral centerpieces pose playful counterpoint to a crisp white art-deco design.

3 C. skinless, boneless chicken breast, diced (or substitute 3 C. shredded rotisserie-style chicken)
¾ teaspoon salt
½ teaspoon black pepper
2 tbsp. vegetable oil, divided
1 onion, thinly sliced
1 red bell pepper, chopped
2 large garlic cloves, thinly sliced
1 C. shredded cheddar cheese
1 C. shredded Monterey Jack cheese (or pepper jack
8 (7-inch) flour tortillas

1. Sprinkle chicken with ½ teaspoon salt and ¼ teaspoon pepper.

2. In a large sauté pan heat 1 tbsp. of oil over medium-high heat. Add the diced chicken and sear until browned. Remove to a bowl and wipe out pan.

3. Add the remaining 1 tbsp. of oil to the pan and cook onion with remaining ¼ teaspoon salt and ¼ teaspoon pepper over medum heat, stirring occasionally, until golden, about 6 minutes.

4. Add red peppers and cook until soft, about 4 minutes, stirring occasionally.

5. Add garlic and cook, stirring, until fragrant, about 1 minute, then transfer onion mixture to a large bowl. Add chicken along with the grated cheeses and gently stir.

6. Place 1 tortilla on a cutting board and spread ½ cup chicken mixture over half of tortilla, then fold other half over to form a half-moon. Repeat with the remaining quesadillas.

7. Heat a lightly oiled grill pan over high heat until it begins to smoke, then reduce heat to medium and grill quesadillas, turning once, until cheese is melted and golden brown grill marks appear, about 4 minutes per batch. Cut in half and serve with sour cream, salsa, fresh cilantro sprigs and fresh lime wedges.

5800 Blue Lagoon Drive, Miami, FL

La Riviera

"I wish my stove came with a Save As button like Word has. That way I could experiment with my cooking and not fear ruining my dinner."
Jarod Kintz

Ham and Turkey Club Sandwich

Serving heavenly sandwiches in Sobe since 1988, La Sandwicherie captures the best of French savoir-faire in the simplest of settings to transport your taste buds to another world without costing you the Earth. Daily fresh ingredients, crisp baguettes or croissants and the added magic of the infamous vinaigrette make for a true taste sensation. A must see in Miami Beach!

6 slices whole wheat bread, toasted
mayonnaise
4 slices ham
4 slices turkey
4 pieces bibb lettuce
2 slices of tomato
4 slices of bacon, cooked crisp
8 toothpicks

1. Begin by spreading mayonnaise on two slices of toast for the base of the sandwich.

2. Top each slice of bread with 1 piece of bibb lettuce and follow with two slices of ham, and two slices of turkey. Break two of the pieces of bacon in half and lay the bacon pieces on top of the turkey.

3. Spread mayonnaise on both sides of two more slices of bread—this will be the middle of the sandwich. Lay the slices of bread on the sandwiches and top with the remaining lettuce. Add 1 slice of tomato to the top of each sandwich. Break the remaining bacon in half and lay the bacon pieces on top of the tomato.

4. Finally, spread mayonnaise on the under side of the remaining pieces of bread and place them on top of each sandwich stack. Use the toothpicks to secure each corner of the sandwich and then cut the sandwich into quarters and serve.

La Sandwicherie
34 Southwest 8th Street, Miami, FL

"Wait. Why am I thinking about Krispy Kremes? We're supposed to be exercising."
Meg Cabot

Onion Soup

Le Bouchon is a friendly little restaurant offering a French Menu and using only the best local products. In the middle of Coconut Grove, as Christian and Jeanne welcome you everyday to a warm and relaxed atmosphere, come and taste our unique cuisine which is a blend of Lyon with a splash of South Florida.

4 tbsp. butter
1 tsp. salt
2 large red onions, thinly sliced
2 large sweet onions, thinly sliced
1 (48-oz.) can chicken broth
1 (14-oz.) can beef broth
½ C. red wine
1 tbsp. Worcestershire sauce
2 sprigs fresh parsley
1 sprig fresh thyme leaves
1 bay leaf
1 tbsp. balsamic vinegar
salt and freshly ground black pepper, to taste
4 thick slices French or Italian bread
8 slices Gruyere or Swiss cheese slices, room temperature
½ C. shredded Asiago or mozzarella cheese, room temperature
4 pinches paprika
2 tbsp. very finely snipped fresh chives

1. Melt butter in a large soup pot over medium-high heat. Stir in salt, red onions and sweet onions. Cook 35 minutes, stirring frequently, until onions are caramelized.

2. Mix chicken broth, beef broth, red wine and Worcestershire sauce into pot. Bundle the parsley, thyme, and bay leaf with twine and place in pot. Simmer over medium heat for 20 minutes, stirring occasionally. Remove and discard the herbs. Reduce the heat to low, mix in vinegar and season with salt and pepper. Cover and keep over low heat to stay hot while you prepare the bread.

3. Preheat oven broiler. Arrange bread slices on a baking sheet and broil 3 minutes, turning once, until well toasted on both sides. Remove from heat; do not turn off broiler.

4. Arrange 4 large oven safe bowls or crocks on a rimmed baking sheet. Fill each bowl ⅔ full with hot soup. Top each bowl with 1 slice toasted bread, 2 slices Gruyere cheese and ¼ of the Asiago or mozzarella cheese. Sprinkle a little bit of paprika over the top of each one.

5. Broil 5 minutes, or until bubbly and golden brown. As it softens, the cheese will cascade over the sides of the crock and form a beautifully melted crusty seal. Serve immediately!

Le Bouchon du Grove
3430 Main Highway, Miami, FL

Omelette Paysanne

Le Boudoir's first location opened in 2005 on the corner of Ponce De Leon and Miracle Mile in Coral Gables, Florida. Our introduction of tableside service and Parisian flair to this affluent town made us the perfect morning, midday and evening complement to the bustling financial and retail district. Guests return to Le Boudoir time and time again not just for authentic French cuisine, but also to enjoy people watching along Coral Gables' most famed retail district. Due to the overwhelming success of the first location, we opened a second spot in what was then seen as the "promising" Brickell area in July 2008.

Signature Taste of MIAMI

2 Idaho potatoes, about ¾ lb.
3 tbsp. peanuts, vegetable or corn oil
Salt & freshly ground pepper to taste
½ C. halved, very thinly sliced onion
1 C. cooked ham, cut into ½" dice
4 tsp. butter
10 eggs
2 tbsp. finely chopped parsley
1 tsp. finely chopped tarragon
2 tsp. finely chopped chives

1. Peel the potatoes and slice them as thinly as possible. Drop into cold water to prevent discoloration. Drain and pat dry.
2. Heat a skillet and add the oil. When it is very hot, add the potatoes. Do not break the slices. Sprinkle with salt and pepper.
3. Cook, making sure the potatoes do not stick. Brown well about 10 minutes and add the onions. Continue cooking about 1 minute. Add the ham and dot with 3 teaspoons of butter. Shake skillet and gently turn over ingredients so that they cook evenly.
4. Beat the eggs with a wire whisk. Add salt, pepper and herbs. Pour the eggs over the ham and potato mixture.
5. Gently stir the mixture from the bottom, allowing the egg mixture to flow to the bottom. Cook over high heat. Lift up the edges of the omelet and let the remaining butter flow beneath the omelet. Shake the skillet to make certain the omelet is loose.
6. Invert a large plate over the skillet and quickly invert the skillet, letting the omelet fall into the plate. This omelet is best served hot, but it is also delicious at room temperature. Also good with crab meat.

186 Southeast 12th Terrace, Miami, FL

Le Boudoir

"There are people in the world so hungry, that God cannot appear to them except in the form of bread."
Mahatma Gandhi

Low Carb Taco

Signature Tastes of MIANI

Crust:
4 oz. cream cheese, softened
3 eggs
⅓ C. heavy cream
½ tsp. taco seasoning
8 oz. cheddar cheese, shredded

Topping:
1 lb ground beef
3 tsp. taco seasoning
¼ C. tomato sauce
4 oz. chopped green chilies
8 oz. cheddar cheese, shredded

1. For the crust, beat the cream cheese and eggs until smooth. Add the cream and seasoning. Grease a 9"x13" baking dish; spread the cheese over the bottom.

2. Pour in the egg mixture as evenly as possible. Bake at 375ºF, 25-30 minutes. Let stand 5 minutes before adding the topping.

3. For the topping, brown the hamburger; drain fat. Stir in the seasoning, tomato sauce and chiles. Spread over the crust. Top with cheese.

4. Reduce oven to 350ºF and bake another 20 minutes or so until hot and bubbly.

5. Serve with the toppings of your choice (add additional carbs).

Lime Fresh Mexican Grill
3201 North Miami Avenue #100 Miami Beach, FL

"If not for me being stoned and clinging to a taco, it would have been terribly romantic."
Richelle Mead, Succubus on Top

Chicken Havana Style

A vibrant Hispanic culture permeates everything in Little Havana, Miami - colorful murals, monuments to heroes past and present, elderly men playing dominoes as they discuss politics, and cigar rollers deeply at work amidst Little Havana's ever-present aroma of Cuban coffee. These scenes of daily Little Havana, Miami life play out amidst a backdrop of Little Havana's pulsating music, vibrant storefronts, unique art galleries and quaint restaurants.

Signature Tastes of MIAMI

4 chicken breast halves
4 chicken thighs
2 Tbsp. minced garlic
2 Tbsp. dried oregano leaves
salt and coarsely-ground black pepper to taste
½ C. red wine vinegar
½ C. extra-virgin olive oil
½ C. currants
½ C. pitted whole Spanish olives
¼ C. capers
3 bay leaves
½ C. firmly-packed brown sugar
½ C. dry white wine
chopped fresh cilantro leaves (for garnish)

1. In a large re-sealable plastic bag, combine garlic, oregano, salt, pepper, wine vinegar, olive oil, currants, Spanish olives, capers, and bay leaves. Add chicken breasts and thighs; seal and let marinate, refrigerated, 12 hours.

2. Preheat oven to 350 degrees F. Place chicken pieces in a 9x13-inch baking dish. Spoon the marinade over the chicken. Sprinkle chicken pieces with brown sugar and carefully pour white wine into the bottom of the pan. Bake 20 to 25 minutes, uncovered, or until a meat thermometer registers an internal temperature of 165 degrees F (juices will run clear when cut with the tip of a knife). Remove from oven.

12727 Biscayne Blvd, North Miami, FL

Little Havana

"Do you know what breakfast cereal is made of? It's made of all those little curly wooden shavings you find in pencil sharpeners!"
Roald Dahl

Lulu
Opening Spring 2010, a new sidewalk cafe in the heart of Coconut Grove
www.luluinthegrove.com
COCONUT GROVE
CBS
ELECTRONICS · HARDWARE
FISHING · BAIT · APPAREL
tackletogo.com 305-854-0005

Fettuccini Carbonara

Lulu is a vision of what an outdoor sidewalk restaurant should be, where commodore meets main highway in the center of coconut grove; a funky neighborhood joint with a sophisticated vibe, a place that will connect people and start a conversation; a meeting venue that will serve dishes to share around a drink. Lulu is the combined effort of individual strengths coming together to create a rhythmic, interplaying, and improvisational masterpiece where each player riffs off his or her own talents and history to bring a fresh, new perspective to the ongoing story.

4-5 rashers bacon, sliced, or 3 cups diced bacon
3 spring onions, diced, or 1 medium onion, sliced
1 x 300 mL cream
1-1½ teaspoons crushed garlic
1 x 200 g punnet sliced mushrooms
1 egg, whisked
1 C. tasty cheese
Fettuccini pasta

1. In a lighly oiled frypan, sauté garlic on a medium heat.

2. Add bacon, mushrooms and onions, and cook for 2 minutes.

3. Add cream and egg, stirring so that egg mixture doesn't thicken and go lumpy.

4. Add cheese to sauce.

5. Pour over the top of cooked pasta.

Lulu in the Grove
3105 Commodore Plaza, Miami, FL

"Am I tough? Am I strong? Am I hard-core? Absolutely. Did I whimper with pathetic delight when I sank my teeth into my hot fried-chicken sandwich? You betcha."
James Patterson

Vito's Veal Parmigiana

Macaluso's is the only restaurant in South Florida that prepares home cooked Italian food from Staten Island, New York. Chef and owner Michael's D'Andrea prepares his family's recipes from 75 years based on family's traditions and recipes from his beloved grandmother Gacomina Macaluso and mother Josephine D'Andrea

2 lb. veal, thinly sliced
Progresso bread crumbs (flavored)
1 lb. Mozzarella (sliced)
1 jar tomato sauce
2 eggs
¼ C. milk (can also use for chicken parmigiana)

1. Mix milk and eggs in bowl. Dip each piece of veal into milk and eggs, then cover with bread crumbs. In frying pan fry each piece lightly, then put in 9x13x2 pan. Put a slice of Mozzarella on each piece and a spoon of sauce (your own or a jar).

2. Bake at 350 degrees until cheese is melted, about 15 minutes.

Macaluso's
1747 Alton Road, Miami, FL

"I cook with wine, sometimes I even add it to the food."
W.C. Fields

Fried Calamari with Tartar Sauce

At Mandolin Aegean Bistro we are proud and passionate about the food we grew up eating. We crave the smell of fresh baked bread, roasted lamb, grilled fish, and of course, our mom's homemade specialties therefore, we're dedicated to recreating dishes that are simple, rustic and authentic to the villages of Greece and Turkey. Our table is where family and friends can gather, for love, for laughter, for spirited conversation, a place to feed your stomach and your soul.

For the Fried Calamari:
1 squid tube
1 egg
1 Tbsp. whole milk
50g breadcrumbs
vegetable oil
1 portion of tartar sauce, recipe below
salt and pepper

For the Tartar Sauce:
250ml mayonnaise (homemade or shop bought)
2 Tbsp. capers
½ red onion
2 Tbsp gherkins
small handful of parsley
2 tsp. whole grain mustard
juice of ½ lemon
salt and pepper

1. Prepare the squid tube by removing the wings, head, innards and backbone (or ask your fishmonger to do this). Wash the squid, pat dry and slice into rings approximately 1 cm wide.

2. Mix the egg and milk and place in a bowl. Make the breadcrumbs by whizzing stale bread slices and place in a bowl along with lots of pepper and a pinch of salt. Cover each ring in the egg mixture, then transfer to the bread-crumbs and coat evenly. Leave to sit for ten minutes before frying.

3. Place 5 cm of oil into a pan and put on high heat with a thermometer until it reaches 180°C.

4. Place one ring at a time into the oil until you have the heat right, it should take 60 seconds per ring. Cook in small batches, remove and lay on kitchen paper to absorb the oil and sprinkle with salt.

Mandolin Aegean Bistro
4312 Northeast 2nd Avenue, Miami, FL

"I've got a sizeable retirement nest egg. It's an ostrich egg, and it's going to make an omelet so big that it'll produce enough leftovers for decades."
Jarod Kintz

Chocolate Peanut Butter Bar

Signature Tastes of MIAMI

Cookie Base:
1 pouch (1 lb 1.5 oz) Betty Crocker double chocolate chunk cookie mix
¼ C. vegetable oil
2 tbsp. cold strong brewed coffee or water
1 egg

Filling:
1 package (8 oz.) cream cheese, softened
¼ C. sugar
1 container (8 oz.) frozen whipped topping, thawed
1 bag (9 oz.) miniature chocolate-covered peanut butter cup candies, chopped

Topping:
¼ C. creamy peanut butter
¼ C. milk
2 tbsp. sugar
3 oz. bittersweet baking chocolate, melted
1 C. unsalted dry-roasted peanuts

1. Heat oven to 350°F. In large bowl, stir cookie base ingredients until soft dough forms. Spread dough in bottom of ungreased 13x9-inch pan. Bake 12 to 15 minutes or just until set. Cool completely, about 30 minutes.

2. In large bowl, beat cream cheese and ¼ cup sugar with electric mixer on medium speed until smooth. Fold in whipped topping and candies. Spread over cooled cookie base.

3. In small microwavable bowl, beat peanut butter, milk and 2 tablespoons sugar with wire whisk until smooth. Microwave uncovered on High 30 to 60 seconds, stirring after 30 seconds, to thin for drizzling. Drizzle mixture over filling. Drizzle with melted chocolate. Sprinkle with peanuts. Refrigerate about 1 hour or until set. For bars, cut into 6 rows by 4 rows. Store covered in refrigerator.

915 Lincoln Road, Miami Beach, FL

Meat Market

"There is no love sincerer than the love of food."
George Bernard Shaw

Chicken Liver Crostini

Michael's Genuine Food & Drink is a showcase for the cuisine of Chef/Owner Michael Schwartz, with prices designed to encourage frequent dining. This unpretentious bistro seats 90 indoors and out, with another 14 seats at a handsome bar. Doubling as a casual neighborhood dining spot and a culinary destination, the bright, airy space in Miami's evolving Design District showcases Schwartz's trademark new American cuisine at prices designed to encourage frequent dining.

Signature Tastes of MIAMI

1 lb. chicken livers
2 tbsp. unsalted butter
¼ C. extra-virgin olive oil
1 white onion, finely chopped
2 sage sprigs
1 rosemary sprig
1 anchovy fillet, minced
1 tbsp. drained capers
Salt and freshly ground pepper
¼ C. cognac
1 large baguette, thinly sliced

1. Trim the chicken livers of any sinews and veins and set them on paper towels to dry for about 20 minutes.

2. Preheat the oven to 350°. In a large skillet, melt the butter in 1 tablespoon of the olive oil. Add the chopped onion, sage and rosemary and cook over moderately high heat, stirring occasionally, until the onion is softened, about 5 minutes.

3. Stir in the minced anchovy and capers and cook over low heat until the onion is lightly browned, about 8 minutes longer. Scrape the mixture into a medium bowl.

4. Add the remaining 3 tablespoons of olive oil to the skillet. Season the chicken livers with salt and pepper, add them to the skillet and cook over high heat until browned, about 2 minutes. Flip and cook the chicken livers for 1 minute longer.

5. Stir in the onion mixture. Add the cognac and carefully ignite it with a long match. Cook the livers until the flames subside.

6. Discard the herb sprigs and scrape the contents of the skillet into a food processor; let cool slightly. Pulse until chunky, then season with salt and pepper.

7. Place the baguette slices on a large baking sheet and toast them for about 15 minutes, until they are golden and crisp. Spread the baguette toasts with the chicken liver and serve.

Michael's Genuine Food & Drink
130 Northeast 40th Street, Miami, FL

"After a good dinner one can forgive anybody, even one's own relatives."
Oscar Wilde

White Gazpacho

Michy's is the golden child restaurant created by husband and wife teamDavid Martinez and Michelle Bernstein. This modern bistro located in the upand coming neigborhood of Miami's "Upper East Side", awakens the 69th block on gritty Biscayne Boulevard withits glowing lights and bustling energy. Chef Bernstein and her team utilizeseasonal ingredients and draw uponlocal farmers and fisherman to create whimsical bistro dishes, a style shecoins as "luxurious comfort food."

2 C. of crustless stale bread, broken into pcs.
2 C. chicken or vegetable stock (use vegetable stock for vegetarian version)
1½ tsp. salt
1 C. slivered blanched almonds (must be blanched, the skins are bitter)
2 C. green seedless grapes, sliced in half
2 cucumbers, peeled, seeded and chopped
1-3 chopped garlic cloves (depending on how garlicky you want the result to be)
2-3 tbsp. sherry vinegar or cider vinegar
¼ C. olive oil
chives for garnish

1. Heat the stock until it's steamy. Turn off the heat and add to the stock the broken up pieces of stale bread. Let cool.

2. Put the almonds, salt and garlic in a food processor and pulse until the almonds are pulverized. Add the soaked bread and any stock that was not absorbed by the bread into the food processor, then add the grapes and cucumbers. Pulse until the mixture is a rough purée.

3. Add 2 tablespoons of the vinegar and pulse a few seconds to combine. Taste and add the other tablespoon if it needs it – grapes can sometimes be acidic enough to leave out the final tablespoon of vinegar.

4. With the motor running, drizzle in the olive oil. Turn off the motor and taste the gazpacho. Add more salt if needed.

5. Chill before serving, garnish with chopped chives.

6927 Biscayne Boulevard Miami, FL

Michy's

"I am a better person when I have less on my plate."
Elizabeth Gilbert

Octopus Carpaccio

Signature Tastes of MIAMI

4 star anise
2 carrots, roughly chopped
2 small white onions, roughly chopped
2 sticks celery, roughly chopped
2 leeks, roughly chopped
1 C. soy sauce
5 cm piece ginger
1 whole large octopus
cardamom seeds, crushed
dill and chervil, to serve

For the lemon and caper dressing:
1 lemon, juice only
1 Tbsp. chopped shallots
1 Tbsp. capers, roughly chopped
4 Tbsp. olive oil

1. In a large stock pot, add all the ingredients, except the octopus, and bring to the boil.

2. Add the octopus and bring back to the boil. Lower the heat and simmer for 40-60 minutes, depending on the size of the octopus.

3. Remove the octopus and drain well.

4. Remove the legs and season well. Lay out the legs on a sheet of clingfilm and roll up tightly. Pierce the finished roll with a sharp knife to allow excess moisture our.

5. Place on a tray and chill for 4-6 hours.

6. Before serving, make the dressing by combining all the dressing ingredients in a bowl and set aside.

Mikan Japanese Restaurant
80 SW 8 Street, Miami, FL

"The only time to eat diet food is while you're waiting for the steak to cook."
Julia Child

Giant Cheesecake Spring Roll

Signature Tastes of MIAMI

Newly opened in a 4,000 square foot space at the 900 Biscayne Bay condo, Miss Yip Chinese Cafe features is traditional Hong Kong fare along with dim sum, dumplings and assorted Chinese snacks. Capitalizing on its enormous space, Miss Yip also aspires to be a downtown nightlife destination with vast outdoor terrace, couches, flat screen TVs, happy hour specials and, for those who just can't be without it, free Wi-Fi.

1 prepared cheese-cake (homemade or store bought)
30 egg roll wraps
1 egg wash (whisk 1 egg with 1 C. of milk)
vegetable oil, as needed
cinnamon sugar, as needed

1. Cut already-baked cheesecake into uniform pieces approximately 1-by-3 inches in size. One large cheesecake will produce about 30 slices for deep frying. Lightly moisten each spring roll wrapper with the egg wash.
2. Blot off excess egg wash with paper towel. Place each piece of cheesecake in the middle of a wrapper. Fold top of wrapper down over the cheesecake, and both sides toward the middle.
3. Roll each piece of cheesecake toward you until it is completely rolled up. Give this "egg roll" a gentle squeeze to make sure the dough is sealed completely. Using a deep frying pan, heat at least 3 inches of oil to 365°F.
4. Dip the corner of one "egg roll" in the heated oil. If the oil sizzles, it is ready. If not, heat the oil a little longer. When the oil is ready, gently release "egg rolls" into the oil and allow to brown lightly, approximately 10 seconds.
5. Using tongs, remove the golden-brown "egg rolls" from the oil. Place each "egg roll" in a bowl of cinnamon sugar and coat well. Place deep-fried slices of cheesecake on paper towels to cool slightly before serving. (I'd use a rack).
6. Caution: These will be very hot. Allow to cool at least 5 minutes before serving. They can be enjoyed warm or cold. (Cinnamon sugar can be made by mixing 2 cups of sugar with 4 tea-spoons of ground cinnamon).

Miss Yip Chinese Café
900 Biscayne Boulevard, Miami, FL

"I'd rather fake my own fog, than fake a steamy love scene. Can I interest you in some mist? It's homemade."
Jarod Kintz

Salmon Ceviche

Moshi Moshi is a fun restaurant to eat, drink and socialize. With 50 succulent tapas appetizers on menu, you will never find it difficult to find the perfect match of tapas to complement 30 selections of premium sake! Moshi Moshi is casual, yet sophisticated. Fun, yet serious. Premium, yet affordable. Ushering you to relatively unknown category of "Izakaya" style of Japanese cuisine, all you have to have yourself to be ready for is open-mindedness.

1 unwaxed lime
1 unwaxed lemon
4 spring onions
1 red chilli
3 tbsp. sesame oil
6 tbsp. olive oil
2 tbsp. soy sauce
1 bunch coriander
1 tsp. caster sugar
750g centre-cut salmon fillet, skin removed
salad leaves, to dress

1. To make the vinaigrette, grate the lime and lemon zest into a bowl - I find using a Microplane is the easiest way to do this but you could use the finest side of a grater. Squeeze the lime and lemon juice into the same bowl as the zest, making sure none of the pips sneak in. Remove the tough outer skins of the spring onions, chop finely and add to the bowl.
2. Roll the chilli between your hands to loosen the seeds. Cut off the top and slice the chilli in half length-wise, scrape out and discard the seeds. Slice length-wise into fine strips, chop finely and add to the bowl. Add the sesame oil, olive oil and soy sauce and mix thoroughly.
3. Now take a handful of coriander leaves (try to avoid the stems) and chop as finely as you can. You need enough to make a good, heaped tablespoon. Add to the bowl and stir. Add a good grind of pepper, pinch of salt and the sugar, stir and that's it, the vinaigrette's ready. You can make this 2 or 3 days ahead if you like.
4. Stretch a couple of sheets of clingfilm taut over a large platter to place the slices of salmon on - this way they won't stick to the surface of the plate and break when you come to dress them. To get neat, even slices the fish needs to be really cold, and you'll need a sharp, unserrated knife. Slice it as soon as it comes out of the fridge or, even better, leave it in the freezer for about 10 minutes before you slice it. Slice the salmon fillet across, aiming for no thicker than 5mm, to give 6 or 7 slices per person. Arrange each slice on the clingfilm.

1448 Washington Avenue, Miami Beach, FL

Moshi Moshi

"Don't wreck a sublime chocolate experience by feeling guilty. Chocolate isn't like premarital sex. It will not make you pregnant. And it always feels good."
Lora Brody

FOR YOUR PROTECTION

All Miami Beach Police Department Officers are authorized
representatives to advise any person to leave these premises.
Failure to vacate the premises after being so instructed may
result in an arrest for trespass after warning

§§ 810.08 & 810.09, FLA. STAT.

POLICE

Cobb Salad

In December of 1998 Mark Soyka and Jeffrey Davis opened News Café, a quaint sidewalk café newsstand and bookstore at the corner of 8th Street and Ocean Drive in the Art Deco District of Miami Beach. The concept was simple: start with a news kiosk and some bookshelves and surround them with tables. Display a selection of local, national and international publications and play a mix of jazz and classical music serve from a basic menu of salads, sandwiches, desserts, fresh fruit juices and coffees.

½ head of romaine
½ head of Boston lettuce
1 small bunch of frisée (curly endive)
½ bunch of watercress, coarse stems discarded
All lettuces should be rinsed, spun or patted dry, and coarsely chopped
6 slices of bacon
2 ripe avocados, seed removed, peeled, and cut into ½-inch pcs.
1 whole skinless bone-less chicken breast (about ¾ lb. total), halved, cooked, and diced
1 tomato, seeded and chopped fine
2 hard-boiled large eggs, separated, the yolk finely chopped and the white finely chopped
2 tbsp. chopped fresh chives
⅓ C. red-wine vinegar
1 tbsp. Dijon-style mustard
1-2 tsp. sugar
Salt and pepper
⅔ C. olive oil
½ C. finely grated Roquefort

1. Cook the bacon in a skillet on medium heat until crisp on both sides. Remove from skillet and lay out on paper towels to absorb the excess fat. Allow the bacon to cool. Crumble the bacon and set aside.

2. In a large salad bowl, toss together well the various lettuces and watercress.

3. Compose the salad. Arrange the chicken, the bacon, the tomato, and the avocado decoratively over the greens and garnish the salad with the grated egg and the chives.

4. In a small bowl whisk together the vinegar, the mustard, and salt and pepper to taste, add the oil in a slow stream, whisking, and whisk the dressing until it is emulsified. Stir in the Roquefort. Add sugar to taste, ½ teaspoon at a time.

5. Whisk the dressing. Serve separately or toss in with the salad.

800 Ocean Drive, Miami Beach, FL

News Café

"Part of the secret of success in life is to eat what you like and let the food fight it out inside."
Mark Twain

Tiramisu

Opened the first restaurant in New York in 1991, Novecento New York Soho, with the objective of bringing new yorkers the authentic taste of argentine cuisine, and make feel at home the argentines traveling to United States. In 1996, he established himself in the Cañitas neighborhood in Buenos Aires, with the idea of reproducing the classic bistro atmosphere of New York. Between 1998 and 2001, Hector opened branches in Martinez (2000), and Punta del Este, Uruguay and Novecento Cordoba, in the historic Cabildo of the city, following in 2005 Novecento Brickell in Miami. In 2007, Novecento Group Holding LLC is finally born, along with strategic partners with the common goal of bringing Novecento to the next commercial phase.

2-3 C. strong plunger espresso coffee, cooled to room temp
3 tbsp. Tia Maria (or another liqueur, but the coffee flavour is really enhanced)
2 eggs, separated
¼ C. caster sugar
250 g mascarpone cheese
1 C. cream (anything that will hold the peaks heavy whipping cream works fine as will anything 36% milkfat or hi)
250 g ladyfingers (savoiardi)
cocoa powder, for dusting

1. Put the egg yolks and sugar in a large bowl. Beat with electric mixers until the mixture goes pale and thick. Add mascarpone and beat until combined. It does not matter if it is marbled slightly.

2. Whip the cream until stiff peaks hold, and fold gently into the egg mixture. I use a spatula, but you could use a metal spoon. Do not beat!

3. Beat the egg whites to soft peaks in a perfectly clean metal bowl. If there is any grease, they won't whip properly. Make sure you rinse and dry your beaters well. Fold the whites into the cream. It is very important to retain as much air as possible.

4. For serving you can use a big dish or individual glasses. If using a big dish: Put the coffee and liquer in a bowl. Dip biscuits in coffee one at a time.

5. Drain well. Layer in your dish, covering the whole bottom. Place half of the mascarpone mix on top and spread out. Repeat with remaining biscuits and mascarpone, finishing with a creamy layer.

6. Smooth surface. Dust with cocoa. Refrigerate for at least 2 hours, but it works quite well if you leave for up to 24 hours.

7. If using glasses: Break the biscuits up into pieces that will fit your glasses and do the same soaking and layering as before.

1414 Brickell Avenue, Miami, FL

Novecento

"What I say is that, if a man really likes potatoes, he must be a pretty decent sort of fellow."
A.A. Milne

Edamame

Argentinian Master Chef Walter Zapata , started his restaurant venture with an Italian restaurant in Buenos Aires at the age of 25. In 2001 he moved to the United State where Walter began looking for work and found a position as a sushi helper in a local restaurant. As his interests in Japanese cuisine began to develop, Walter took on the duty of Sushi Chef in an Authentic Japanese restaurant to expand his experience. Soon after Walter met his wife Erika Ramirez – who is also a Sushi Chef at OBBA- and his business partner Tufic Akil.

8 oz. fresh soybeans in the pod
course salt/sea salt
fresh ground pepper

1. Fill a large pot with an inch or so of water and insert a steaming basket/insert.

2. Place the soybeans in the basket/insert and bring the water to a boil. Steam the pods for about 5 minutes.

3. Remove the basket/insert and rinse the beans under cold water for just a few seconds. Drain.

4. Sprinkle with salt and pepper and consume.

Obba Sushi
200 Southeast 15th Road, Miami, FL

"I am not a glutton - I am an explorer of food"
Erma Bombeck

Johnny O's Famous Bagels

Offerdahl's goes beyond just bagels and other baked goods, offering a wide variety of specialty salads and sandwiches that keep the lunch crowds happy. The grilled chicken sandwich featuring Footy's special tropical barbecue sauce is a favorite, as are the array of Asian-themed noodle bowls.

Dough:
1½ C. warm water (110 to 115*F / 45*C)
1 tbsp. dry active yeast
1 tbsp. sugar
1 tbsp. vegetable oil
2 tsp. salt
4½ C. unbleached bread flour (more if needed)

Kettle Water:
6 qrts water
1 tsp. salt

Toppings:
sesame seeds
poppy seeds
caraway seeds
coarse salt
corn meal

1. In a large mixing bowl, stir together water, yeast, and sugar. Let stand for 5 minutes.
2. With a wooden spoon, stir in oil and one cup of the flour. Add salt, then enough of remaining flour to make a stiff dough.
3. On a lightly floured surface, knead for 10 to 12 minutes. Cover with a floured dish towel and allow dough to rest on a board for about 15 minutes.
4. Divide dough into 8 sections and form each section into 10-inch long strips. Roll the ends together to seal and make a ring. Place on a lightly floured surface, cover, and let bagels rest 15 to 20 minutes, rising about halfway and becoming slightly puffy.
5. Meanwhile, fill a large cooking pot or Dutch oven three quarters full with water. Add the salt.
6. Bring water to a boil. Preheat oven to 450 degrees F. Line a large jelly roll pan with baking parchment and set aside.
7. Line another jelly roll pan with a kitchen towel, set near your stove. Reduce boiling water to a simmer and cook 2 bagels at a time (do not crowd the pot). Simmer bagels for about 45 seconds on one side, then turn and cook other side for another 45 seconds and then drain bagels on the towel-lined baking sheet.
8. Dip bagel into corn meal so that the bottom is covered, then set on parchment-lined jelly roll pan. Make up an egg wash (2 eggs, beaten) and brush tops of bagels with egg. If you want seed toppings, then immediately after applying egg wash sprinkle poppy seeds or sesame seeds on the bagels. If you don't do it right away, the egg will dry and the seeds will simply fall off.
9. Carefully place bagels on the parchment-lined baking sheets. The original recipe called for six bagels on the baking sheet, but I would place all 8 bagels on the jelly roll pan. Place in the hot oven, immediately reduce heat to 425 degrees F, and bake about 17 to 25 minutes. Transfer bagels to wire rack to cool.

Offerdahl's Café Grill
195 Southeast 3rd Avenue, Miami, FL

"I had a missed call. It's probably the all you can eat buffet calling to say, 'Come back! We know you can eat just a little bit more.'"
Jarod Kintz

Mixto Ceviche

OLA's wine list has been carefully chosen, by Sommelier Albert O'Mahen to compliment the bold flavors of Chef Rivadero's menu. Our sommelier will introduce you to exciting varietals from Spain and South America and across the globe. OLA Restaurant is located in the cool comfort of the Sanctuary Hotel, 1745 James Ave, walking distance from Lincoln Road and South Beach's most luxurious resorts and hotels. Rooftop dining is available for private parties and large groups. Chef Horacio Rivadero was named recently by Food and Wine Magazine as" Best New Chef for the Gulf Region 2012" and the restaurant was named by Zagat as "Extrodinary for food with a 27 rating".

Signature Tastes of MIAMI

7 oz. octopus, cooked
shrimp, tails
blanched
7 oz. scallops
1 red onion, sliced
very fine
½ red aji limo chile,
minced
½ yellow aji limo
chile, minced
16 key limes, juice of
salt
2 sweet potatoes,
boiled (camote
variety, if you can
get it)
1 large fresh ear corn
on the cob, cooked
and cut into rounds
(choclo variety, if you
can get it)

1. Cut octopus into bite-size pieces. Leave whole if using baby octopus.

2. Cut squid into small rings.

3. Mix seafood with onion in large bowl. Wash and drain thoroughly.

4. Season mixture with salt and aji limo chiles.

5. Toss preparation quickly in lime juice. Refresh with ice cubes, mixing well. Remove ice immediately before it has a chance to melt.

6. Serve on bed of lettuce with sweet potato (camote, if you can get it) and boiled corn rounds (choclo, if you can get it).

1745 James Avenue, Miami Beach, FL

OLA

"We must have a pie. Stress cannot exist in the presence of a pie."
David Mamet

Salada de Polvo

Welcome to a Portuguese Gourmet Experience! The flavor of Portugal first delights your senses with the aroma emanating from the traditional open kitchen surrounded by Old World Decor. You sample our delicacies, pamper your senses, and when you feel compelled to stop, we tempt you with our extravagant desserts. We help you select your gourmet experience from our culinary repertoire and our extensive wine and Port list.

400 g octopus
1 medium onion
150 g Pickles
(cauliflower,
cucumber and carrot)
few drops of olive oil
few drops of vinegar

1. Rinse the octopus and place in a pan. Cover the pan and cook (without water) on medium heat, until tender.

2. Drain the octopus and cut into small pieces.

3. Finely chop the onion and pickles.

4. Combine octopus pieces, onion, and pickles in a large serving bowl.

5. Drizzle few drops of olive oil and vinegar.

6. Toss to mix thoroughly and serve.

Old Lisbon Restaurant
1698 Southwest 22nd Street, Miami, FL

"Hydrogenated and androgynous milky white love is all I have to offer you. Would you like me to pour it in your coffee, or directly into your soul?"
Jarod Kintz

Argentinean Beef Empanadas

Olivos Restaurant pleased the most delight palate. When you're in the mood for good times and great cuisine, be sure to check out Olivos. The restaurant is located in one of the area's most pleasant settings and is known for its delightful staff and superb cuisine. The menu at Olivos features a wide array of great selections, made from only the freshest and highest quality ingredients, with something sure to please every member of your group. Olivos has established itself as one of the area's favorite culinary destinations and is sure to offer you a pleasant and unique dining experience every time you visit.

Dough:
2 C. all-purpose flour
1-2 tsp. Salt
¾ C. cold margarine or ¾ C. butter, cut into small cubes
2 eggs
⅔ C. cold water
2 Tbsp. white vinegar

Meat Filling:
1 lb ground beef (or turkey or chicken for a lower-fat variation)
4 hard-boiled eggs
1 C. stuffed green olive
handful raisins (optional. This is supposedly a common ingredient, but I have never used them)
1 large onion
3 garlic cloves
2 -3 Tbsp. ground cumin powder
1 tsp. chili pepper flakes
1-2 Tbsp. sugar salt and pepper

1. Sift the flour, mix the sifted flour and salt in a large bowl.
2. Mix in the solid margarine or butter with your fingers, (best to cross cut with two knives). The flour should have an even, coarse texture, with the margarine lumps no larger than a pea.
3. Beat together the water, eggs, and vinegar in a bowl. Slowly mix into the flour mixture, until you have the desired consistency (it should not be too sticky, but still malleable).
4. Place the mixture on a floured surface. Knead with the heel of your hand to bring the dough together.
5. Cover the dough and allow to sit in a cool place for at least an hour.
6. Roll out the dough until it is about 1/8 of an inch (0.3 cm) thick. Cut into circles about 4-6 inches (10 - 15 cm) in diameter and lightly flour them.
7. Heat some oil in a large saucepan. Mince the onions and garlic, and add to the pan. Cook until the onions become translucent.
8. Add the ground meat. Break it up with with a spoon and cook, stirring until lightly browned. Drain off fat.
9. Mix in the cumin, pepper flakes, and sugar. Adjust to taste.
10. Chop the hard boiled eggs and halve the stuffed olives. Carefully mix into the meat mixture. Add salt and pepper to taste.
11. Preheat the oven to 375ºF/200ºC.
12. Stuff the empanada dough wrappers. Place 2-3 tablespoons of the filling in the center of each wrapper. Dampen the outer perimeter of the dough.
13. Fold over, forming a semicircle. Pinch a corner of the dough, and then fold that section onto itself. Pinch and pull out another ½-inch (1.2 cm) section and fold over, so that it slightly overlaps the first piece. Repeat along the length of the folded side, until you create a braided or twisted seal.
14. If desired, brush the tops of the empanadas with beaten egg yolk for a nice golden color.
15. Place the folded empanadas on a greased cookie sheet. Bake 15-20 minutes, or until golden brown.

10455 Northwest 41st Street, Doral, FL

Olivos Restaurant

"There is one thing more exasperating than a wife who can cook and won't, and that's a wife who can't cook and will."
Robert Frost

Rigatoni Amatriciana

Everything has been homemade for the last 20 years at this award-wining Italian Restaurant, which is tucked inside the stylish Art Deco District of South Beach. The intimate dining room is comfortable and elegant, and the small size makes you feel like you have made a special secret discovery. The excellent staff will always make you feel at home as you enjoy succulent seafood, fresh al dente pasta, tongue-tingling sauces and hearty just-baked bread.

1 package (16 oz. size) rigatoni pasta
¼ C. extra virgin olive oil
1 clove garlic, minced
½ tsp. crushed red pepper flakes, or to taste
1½ C. chopped onion
oz. pancetta or bacon, cut into thin strips
¾ C. dry white wine
16 oz. plum tomatoes, peeled seeded and chopped
salt and pepper, to taste
1 C. freshly grated Romano cheese

1. Cook rigatoni according to package directions; drain and return to pot.

2. Meanwhile, heat oil in large skillet over low heat. Saute garlic and red pepper 4 minutes or until garlic is golden. Remove garlic and discard.

3. Add onions to skillet and cook over medium heat about 8 minutes until golden, stirring frequently. Add pancetta and cook 5 minutes, stirring frequently.

4. Add wine and bring to boiling. Cook until wine is almost evaporated, about 8 minutes. Stir in tomatoes and cook 5 minutes until slightly thickened. Season to taste with salt and pepper.

5. Stir tomato mixture into rigatoni. Toss gently with cheese. Transfer to serving platter.

Osteria del Teatro

1443 Washington Avenue, Miami Beach, FL

"How can you govern a country which has 246 varieties of cheese?"
Charles de Gaulle

Filet Mignon

Otentic is a friendly and cozy restaurant that makes you feel at home. The chef creates otentic (authentic) fresh french food with his knowledge and experience brought from the capital of food, Paris. You can delight every day specials and a la carte meals in the restaurant located in heart of South Beah or delivered at home.

3 Tbsp. unsalted butter
1 lb. mixed wild mushrooms, such as shiitake and cremini, trimmed
kosher salt and freshly ground pepper
4 (6-oz) beef fillets, about 1½ in. thick
1 shallot, finely chopped
2 Tbsp. grainy mustard
1 C. heavy cream
2 Tbsp. chopped fresh flat-leaf parsley, plus more for garnish, optional

1. Heat 2 tablespoons butter in a large, heavy nonstick skillet over medium-high heat until hot. Add the mushrooms and ½ teaspoon salt and ½ teaspoon pepper. Cook, stirring occasionally, until browned, about 6 minutes.

2. Wipe out the skillet. Heat the remaining 1 tablespoon butter in the skillet over high heat until hot. Sprinkle the beef generously with salt and pepper. Sear over medium-high heat, turning once halfway through, until browned, about 12 minutes for medium. Transfer the beef to a platter.

3. Add the shallots to the skillet and cook over medium heat, stirring, until golden, about 3 minutes. Add the mustard and heavy cream and bring to a boil, cooking until slightly thickened, about 3 minutes. Stir in the parsley. Spoon the sauce on a plate; place the beef on the sauce and scatter the mushrooms over top. Garnish with additional parsley, if desired.

710 Washington Ave. Suite3 South Beach, Miami, Fl

Otentic

"The only real stumbling block is fear of failure. In cooking you've got to have a what-the-hell attitude."
Julia Child

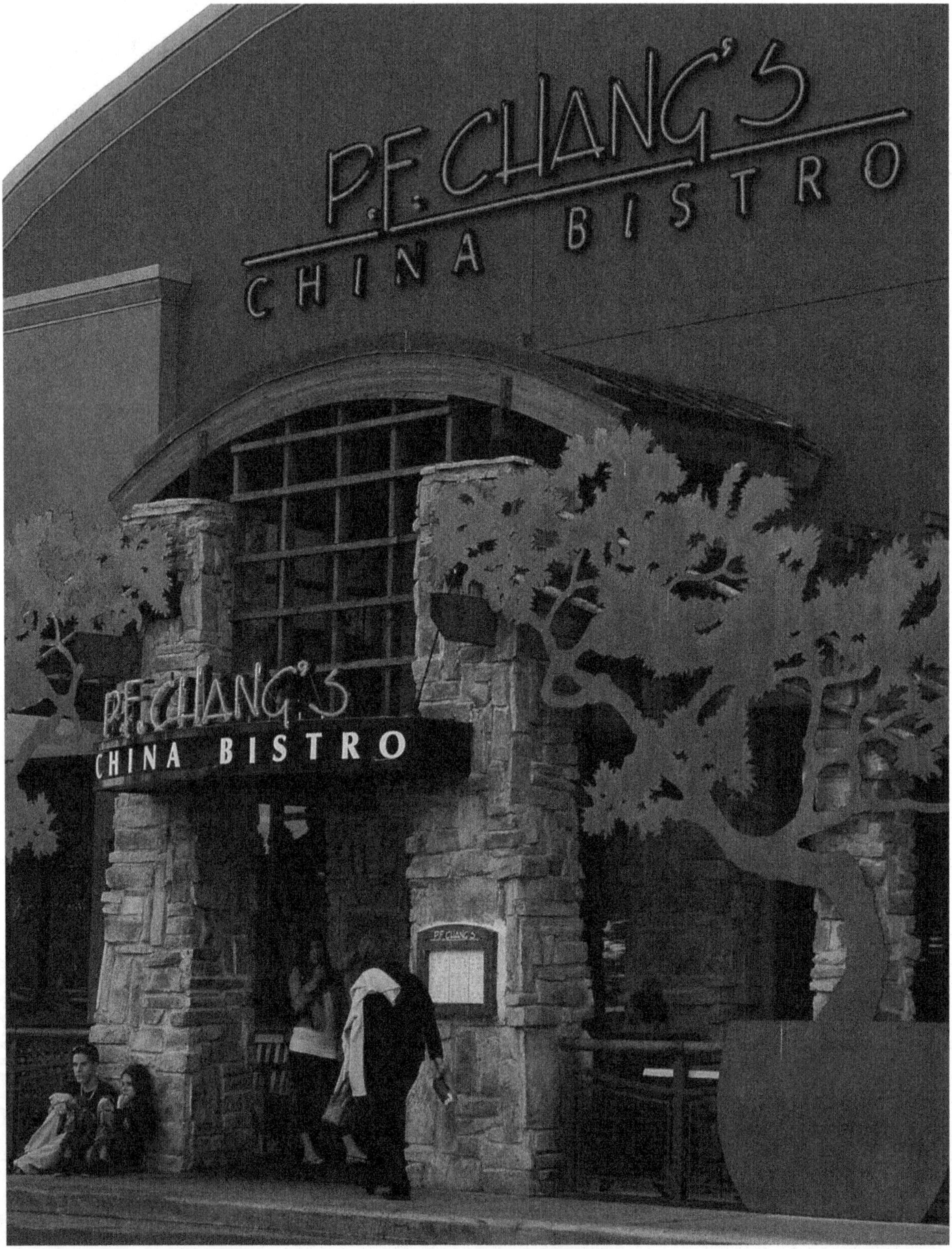
P.F. CHANG'S
CHINA BISTRO
P.F. CHANG'S
CHINA BISTRO
P.F. CHANG'S

Grilled Chicken Chopped Salad

P.F. Chang's China Bistro is a wonderfully casual restaurant with great food and excellent service. Located at The Falls shopping mall at Dixie Highway and SW 130th Street, it is a great way to relax after a day of shopping. Although the parking at The Falls can be difficult sometimes, this eatery is worth it!

1 lb. skinless, boneless chicken thighs, timmed of fat
2 tsp. vegetable oil
1 tsp. lower-sodium fish sauce
3 tbsp. lower-sodium fish sauce
.25 C. fresh lime juice
1 clove garlic, crushed with press
.5 tsp. light brown sugar
.25 tsp. Asian chili sauce (Sriracha)
1 head green cabbage, trimmed and cored
1 medium red onion
3 hearts romaine lettuce
.5 C. packed fresh cilantro leaves, plus additional for garnish
.5 C. packed fresh mint leaves, plus additional for garnish
3 tbsp. roasted unsalted peanuts

1. Heat large ridged grill pan on medium until hot. In large bowl, toss chicken thighs with vegetable oil and 1 teaspoon fish sauce until evenly coated.

2. Working in batches if necessary, cook chicken 7 to 9 minutes or until juices run clear when pierced with tip of knife, turning once. Transfer chicken to plate. Cool slightly; cut into ½-inch chunks.

3. Meanwhile, in large bowl, whisk lime juice, garlic, sugar, chili sauce, and remaining fish sauce until combined. Thinly slice cabbage and add to bowl with dressing. Toss to coat evenly. Let stand while preparing remaining ingredients.

4. Meanwhile, thinly slice onion and coarsely chop lettuce, cilantro, and mint; add to bowl with cabbage. Chop peanuts and add to bowl, along with chicken and any juices. Toss to combine. Garnish with additional cilantro and mint.

P.F. Chang's China Bistro
17455 Biscayne Boulevard, North Miami Beach, FL

"Eat food. Not too much. Mostly plants."
Michael Pollan

Spinach Omelette

Signature Tastes of MIAMI

Brickell is home to Miami and South Florida's financial district as well as the site of many new high-rise luxury condominium and office towers that constantly redefine the Miami skyline. Referred to as the Manhattan of the South, Upper Brickell is home to the largest concentration of international banks in the United States. In 2004 Dr. Arthur Agatston published its successful South Beach Diet Cook Book with recipes from a select handful upscale restaurants from New York and Miami. Pasha's is the only fast casual restaurant to be part of this selection. The book which became a New York Times Best Seller with over $3 million books sold worldwide proclaimed "Pasha's serves healthy and delicious Mediterranean food, proving once again the two are never mutually exclusive"

2 medium plum tomatoes
2 oz. feta cheese
2 C. (loosely packed) baby spinach leaves
8 large eggs
½ C. water
½ tsp. salt
½ tsp. coarsely ground black pepper
2 tbsp. margarine or butter
Toasted country-style bread (optional)

1. Chop tomatoes. Crumble feta cheese. Thinly slice spinach leaves

2. Preheat oven to 200 degrees F. Place 4 dinner plates in oven to warm. In medium bowl, place eggs, water, salt, and black pepper. With fork, beat 25 to 30 quick strokes to blend mixture without making it fluffy. (Overbeating toughens the proteins in the whites.)

3. In 8-inch nonstick skillet, melt 1½ teaspoons margarine on medium. When margarine stops sizzling, pour or ladle ½ cup egg mixture into skillet.

4. After egg mixture begins to set around edges, about 25 to 30 seconds, with heat-safe spatula, carefully push cooked egg from side of skillet toward center, so uncooked egg can reach bottom of hot skillet. Repeat 8 to 10 times around skillet, tilting as necessary, 1 to 1 ½ minutes.

5. Cook until omelet is almost set but still creamy and moist on top. Place skillet handle facing you, and layer one-fourth of crumbled feta, spinach leaves, and chopped tomatoes over half of each omelet.

6. With spatula, fold unfilled half over filling.

7. Shake pan gently to loosen any egg or filling from edge, then slide omelet to edge of skillet. Holding skillet above warm plate, tip skillet so omelet slides onto plate. Keep warm in oven. Repeat with remaining margarine, egg mixture, tomatoes, spinach, and feta to make 4 omelets in all.

8. Serve with toast and a mixed greens salad with balsamic vinaigrette if you like.

900 Lincoln Road, South Beach Miami, FL

Pasha's

"The most remarkable thing about my mother is that for thirty years she served the family nothing but leftovers. The original meal has never been found."
Calvin Trillin

Never Too Sweet

Fougasse

Signature Tastes of MIAMI

PAUL opens its first bakery outside France, in Barcelona. It is the begining of our international development. Two years late, some bakeries incorporate a cafe area and or a restaurant. Francis Holder decided to re-energise PAUL and added two new components to the business; the now famous black shop fronts and the development of a rustic line of specialty breads using sustainably produced winter wheat. PAUL celebrates its 120 year anniversary renewing the companies commitment to providing fresh bread, baked daily using traditional, time-honored methods by introducing the « Charlemagne » baguette to honor our founder Charlemagne Mayot. PAUL continues to be be a family owned company built on the foundions of time-honored production methods passed down through five generations.

For starter:
1 tsp. sugar
½ C. warm water (105–115°F)
2 tsp. active dry yeast (from a ¼-oz. package)
½ C. all-purpose flour

For dough:
2 tbsp. sugar
1 ¼ tsp. table salt
1 tsp. anise seeds, lightly crushed
⅔ C. water
2 tsp. orange-flower water (preferably French)
1 tsp. finely grated fresh orange zest
⅓ C. mild extra-virgin olive oil (preferably French) plus 1 tbsp. for brushing
3 ¼ C. unbleached all-purpose flour plus additional for kneading

Make starter:
1. Stir together sugar and warm water in bowl of mixer. Sprinkle yeast over mixture and let stand until foamy, about 5 minutes. (If yeast doesn't foam, discard and start over with new yeast.)
2. Whisk flour into yeast mixture until combined well. Let starter rise, loosely covered with plastic wrap, 30 minutes.

Make dough:
1. Add sugar, salt, crushed anise seeds, water, orange-flower water, zest, ⅓ cup oil, and 1 ¼ cups flour to starter and beat at medium speed until smooth. Mix in remaining 2 cups flour, ½ cup at a time, at low speed until a soft dough forms.
2. Turn dough out onto a lightly floured surface and knead, sprinkling surface lightly with flour if dough is very sticky, until smooth and elastic (dough will remain slightly sticky), 8 to 10 minutes. Form dough into a ball and transfer to a lightly oiled large bowl, turning dough to coat with oil. Cover bowl with plastic wrap and let dough rise in a draft-free place at warm room temperature until doubled in bulk, 1 to 1½ hours.
3. Punch down dough (do not knead), then halve. Pat out each half into an oval (about 12 inches long and ¼ inch thick), then transfer to 2 lightly oiled large baking sheets.
4. Using a very sharp knife or a pastry scraper, make a cut down center of each oval "leaf," cutting all the way through to baking sheet and leaving a 1-inch border on each end of cut. Make 3 shorter diagonal cuts on each side of original cut, leaving a 1-inch border on each end of cuts, to create the look of leaf veins (do not connect cuts).
5. Gently pull apart cuts about 1 ½ inches with your fingers. Let dough stand, uncovered, until slightly puffed, about 30 minutes.
6. Put oven racks in upper and lower thirds of oven and pre-heat oven to 375°F.
7. Brush loaves with remaining tablespoon oil and sprinkle with sea salt. Bake, switching position of baking sheets halfway through baking, until loaves are golden brown and sound hollow when tapped on bottom, 35 to 40 minutes total.
8. Transfer loaves to a rack and cool to warm or room temperature.

Paul Maison de Qualite
19575 Biscayne Boulevard Aventura, FL

"Anything is good if it's made of chocolate."
Jo Brand

Almond Joy

From the day it opened its doors for the first time on June 1, 1994 - the Pelican has been the coolest hotel in the heart of South Beach. The $4million dollar Fellini-esque boutique property is the first hotel venture from the cutting-edge Diesel Jeans. It works because; it uniquely and wonderfully brings to life the Diesel philosophy. The quirky, surreal, state-of-the-art sense of humor the identity of the hugely successful Italian clothing conglomerate comes through in every pore of the Pelican.

1 tbsp. apple cider
1 tbsp. cider vinegar
2 tsp. fresh lemon juice
1 tsp. dijon-style mustard
1 tbsp. shallot (minced)
½ tsp. worcestershire sauce
⅛ tsp. dried thyme (crumbled)
¼ C. vegetable oil
1½ red delicious apples
2 belgian endives (inches cut from the tips and reserved for garnish and the remainder cut cross-wise into ½ inch thick slices)
6 C. watercress (loosely packed, sprigs rinsed and spun dry)
3 tbsp. sliced almonds (crumbled)

1. In a bowl whisk together the cider, the vinegar, the lemon juice, the mustard, the shallot, the Worcestershire sauce, the thyme, and salt and pepper to taste, add the oil in a stream, whisking, and whisk the dressing until it is emulsified.

2. Let the dressing stand at room temperature for 30 minutes to let the flavors develop. In another bowl toss the apples, cored and cut into ½-inch pieces, with 2 tablespoons of the dressing.

3. In a large bowl toss together the endive slices and the watercress with the remaining dressing and divide the watercress mixture among the 6 salad plates. Top the watercress with the apples and the almonds and garnish the plates with the reserved endive tips.

Pelican Café
826 Ocean Drive, Miami Beach, FL

"Give a man a fish, and you'll feed him for a day. Teach a man to fish, and he'll buy a funny hat. Talk to a hungry man about fish, and you're a consultant."
Scott Adams

Goat Cheese Salad

Perricone's is a great alternative to the hustle, bustle and high prices of nearby South Beach. Located near Brickell Avenue in Mary Brickell Village, Perricone's is surrounded by downtown Miami hotels, making it easy to incorporate a visit to Perricone's while you're on vacation or just taking a short weekend getaway. Perricone's is also Miami's best gourmet market stocked with fine wines, indulgent coffees and teas and decadent desserts. On any day of the week, you can take advantage of Perricone's many specials aimed at making your palette and pocketbook feel great! The restaurant even offers free Wi-Fi services for busy computer-savvy patrons looking to connect to the Internet quickly.

For the salad:
2 small handfuls snap pea pods, trimmed
4 oz. goat cheese (plain or flavored), rolled into cherry tomato-sized balls and chilled
1 large egg, beaten
1 C. panko bread-crumbs
3 C. mixed salad greens, washed and dried
4 radishes sliced paper-thin on a mandoline or v-slicer

For the Pecan-Fennel Vinaigrette:
¼ C. white wine vinegar
2 tbsp. Dijon mustard
1 clove garlic
¼ tsp. fennel seeds
½ tsp. salt
½ tsp. freshly ground black pepper
1 C. high-quality extra virgin olive oil
¼ C. pecans, toasted

For the Pecan-Fennel Vinaigrette:
1. Combine all ingredients in a blender until smooth.

For the Goat Cheese:
1. Dunk each ball into the egg and roll lightly in breadcrumbs. Chilling them beforehand will help them keep their round shape. When all the goat cheese is breaded, return to refrigerator until ready to fry.
2. When ready, preheat fryer to 350, drop in goat cheese and fry for 2-3 minutes, or until deep golden brown. Remove with a slotted spoon and drain on a layer of paper towels.

For the Salad:
1. In a pot of salted boiling water, blanch the snap peas for about a minute until bright green, then transfer with a slotted spoon to a bowl of ice water until cool, drain and set aside.
2. Plate salad greens with pea pods and radishes and freshly fried goat cheese.
3. Drizzle with pecan-fennel vinaigrette and serve immediately.

Perricone Marketplace & Cafe Miami
15 Southeast 10th Street, Miami, FL

"Ice-cream is exquisite. What a pity it isn't illegal."
Voltaire

Classic Caesar Salad

To keep it short..."THE BEST PIZZA YOU'VE EVER HAD", delivered hot and crispy to your home in around 30 minutes or less. Our pizza's and salads are made using only the best, mostly organic products such as Italian plum tomato sauce, Vermont organic flour, Winscosin gourmet chesses (a couple hail from California as well), and so much more. Pieducks was born from an immense passion for great pizza, speedy delivery, a commitment for excellent service and e desire to provide a healthy alternative to what we call "Junk Pizza". We are expanding quick, but for now you can find us with the best tasting pizza delivery in Miami... Try us, we are sure you will agree.

For The Croutons:
2 tbsp. unsalted butter, melted
1 tbsp. extra-virgin olive oil
1 loaf rustic Italian bread (8 to 10 oz.), crusts removed, cut into ¼-inch cubes
2 tsp. salt
¼ tsp. ground cayenne pepper
½ tsp. freshly ground black pepper

For the Salad:
2 garlic cloves
4 anchovy fillets
1 tsp. salt
1 tsp. freshly ground pepper
1 tbsp. freshly squeezed lemon juice
1 tsp. Worcestershire sauce
½ tsp. Dijon mustard
1 large egg yolk
½ C. extra-virgin olive oil
20 oz. romaine lettuce, outer leaves discarded, inner leaves washed and dried
1 C. freshly grated Parmesan cheese or Romano cheese, or 2½ oz. shaved with a vegetable peeler

1. Preheat oven to 450 degrees. Combine the butter and olive oil in a large bowl. Add the cubes of read, and toss until coated. Sprinkle with salt, cayenne pepper, and black pepper; toss until evenly coated. Spread the bread in a single layer on a 12-by-17-inch baking sheet. Bake until croutons are golden, about 10 minutes. Set aside.

2. Place the garlic, anchovy fillets, and salt in a wooden salad bowl. Using two dinner forks, mash the garlic and anchovies into a paste. Using one fork, whisk in the pepper, lemon juice, Worcestershire sauce, mustard, and egg yolk. Whisk in the olive oil.

Pieducks

1451 South Miami Avenue, Miami, FL

"You can't just eat good food. You've got to talk about it too. And you've got to talk about it to somebody who understands that kind of food."
Kurt Vonnegut

Margherita Pizza

In 1986, in the heart of Treviso, a new idea takes shape: the re-invention of the most quintessential Italian establishment: the Pizzeria, that idea is now a wonderful reality called Piola. The success achieved in Italy by Piola has started to spread around the world: Piola's quality is now sought after by discriminating and trend-setting international clientele in the United States, Brazil, Argentina, Chile, Mexico, Turkey and Honduras. At Piola, the most genuine Italian tradition of simple and delicious food combines cleverly with a particular service and ambiance for the demanding and modern customer, who chooses Piola aware of the fact that feeling comfortable is as important as eating well. People from all walks of life and backgrounds meet and gather at Piola, since they are sure to find their own space in an atmosphere that balances freedom and well being with good taste.

¼ C. olive oil
1 tbsp. minced garlic
½ tsp. sea salt
8 Roma tomatoes, sliced
2 (12 inch) pre-baked pizza crusts
8 oz. shredded Mozzarella cheese
4 oz. shredded Fontina cheese
10 fresh basil leaves, washed, dried
½ C. freshly grated Parmesan cheese
½ C. crumbled feta cheese

1. Stir together olive oil, garlic, and salt; toss with tomatoes, and allow to stand for 15 minutes. Preheat oven to 400 degrees F (200 degrees C).

2. Brush each pizza crust with some of the tomato marinade. Sprinkle the pizzas evenly with Mozzarella and Fontina cheeses. Arrange tomatoes overtop, then sprinkle with shredded basil, Parmesan, and feta cheese.

3. Bake in preheated oven until the cheese is bubbly and golden brown, about 10 minutes.

1250 South Miami Avenue, Miami, FL

Piola

"I am at the moment writing a lengthy indictment against our century. When my brain begins to reel from my literary labors, I make an occasional cheese dip."
John Kennedy Toole

Tomato Basil Pizza

Signature Tastes of MIAMI

In May 1996, Pizza Rustica opened its doors on the corner of 9th Street and Washington in Miami Beach, Florida. Customers were lured in by the aroma of fresh pizzas baking. They had never seen these Roman-style rectangular pans of pizza with so many unique gourmet toppings. Word began to spread among locals and tourists alike that Pizza Rustica was the place where everyone loved to come and enjoy a fast and affordable gourmet meal.

12-inch prepared pizza dough
cornmeal for dusting
extra-virgin olive oil for brushing
6 plum tomatoes, peeled, seeded and diced, or ¼ C. tomato sauce
⅓ lb. mozzarella cheese, thinly sliced
Salt and freshly ground pepper, to taste
8 fresh basil leaves, torn into ½-inch pcs.

1. Place a cast-iron pizza pan in an oven and preheat to 450ºF.

2. Roll out the dough into a 12-inch round. Lightly dust a baking peel with cornmeal and lay the dough on top. Lightly brush the dough with olive oil and spread the tomatoes evenly on top, leaving a ½-inch border. Lay the cheese slices evenly over the tomatoes. Season with salt and pepper.

3. Carefully slide the pizza onto the preheated pizza pan. Bake until the bottom of the crust is golden and the cheese is bubbly, about 15 minutes. Remove the pan from the oven and sprinkle the pizza with the basil. Let cool for 5 minutes before serving. Serves 2.

863 Washington Avenue, Miami Beach, FL

Pizza Rustica

"Blood may be thicker than water, but it's certainly not as thick as ketchup. Nor does it go as well with French fries."
Jarod Kintz

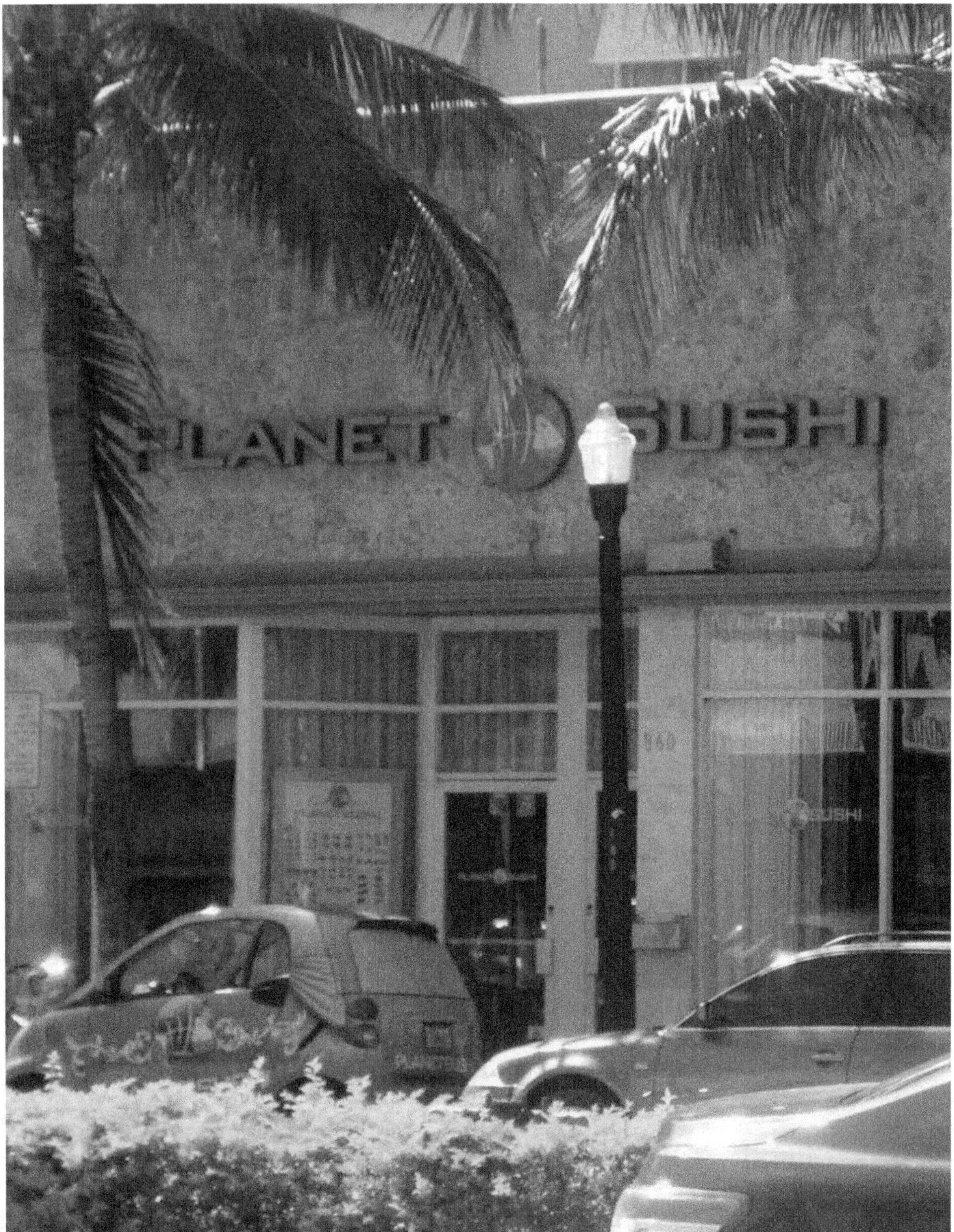
PLANET SUSHI

Eby Fry

Signature Tastes of MIAMI

Planet Sushi Miami is a modern Japanese restaurant group known for its ample portions and striking designs. Started in 1998 by Siben N'Ser, a french entrepreneur, the group has now 26 restaurants, 42 under development, 680 employee, 280 scooters for delivery and more than 250 products on the menu. Planet Sushi serves inventive Japanese cuisine ranging from sushi, sashimi and creative fusion food to signature dishes like maki foie gras, maki slim, red slim, smoki, jb tempura, tartares, specialty rolls. Planet Sushi also provides delivery and catering services, private rooms and lounges, outdoor dining spaces and a vibrant bar scene.

Few big prawn (Black Tiger prawn)
¼ tsp. baking soda
1 tbsp. corn starch
1 egg white (beaten)
1 egg (add with 1 table spoon water and beat the egg)
¼ C. flour
Panko breadcrumbs
Oil for frying

1. Remove the prawn head , shell and vein, but leave the tail part.
2. Soak clean prawn in ice water add with baking soda for about 30 minutes.
3. Rinse prawn with running water , drain the water and beaten egg white and corn starch and lightly massage the prawn for about 1 – 2 minutes.
4. Again, rinse the prawn and dry with paper towel.
5. Make diagonal cut on prawn bottom and press the prawn on the back to ensure prawn won't curl up during frying process.
6. Roll prawn on flour until evenly coated , shake the excess flour and then dip in beaten egg.
7. Roll the prawn on panko until evenly coated.
8. Then dip the panko coated prawn into egg mixture again and then roll on panko again, shake to remove the excess panko.
9. Deep fry the prawn until golden yellow and crispy, remove and drain on paper towel.

860 Washington Avenue, Miami Beach, FL

Planet Sushi

"I breathe in slowly. Food is life. I exhale, take another breath. Food is life. And that's the problem. When you're alive, people can hurt you. It's easier to crawl into a bone cage or a snowdrift of confusion. It's easier to lock everybody out. But it,s a lie."
Laurie Halse Anderson

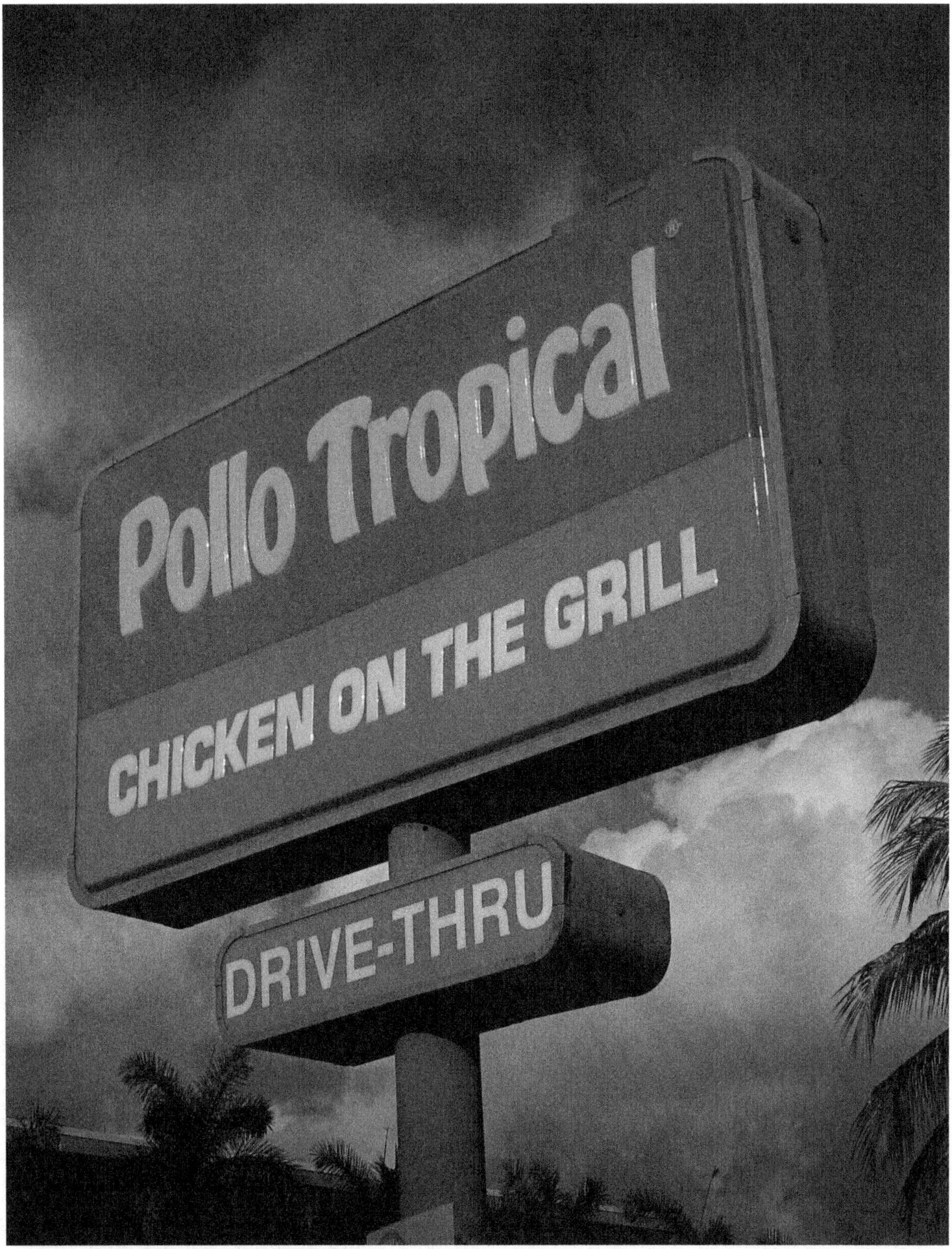

Pollo Tropical®
CHICKEN ON THE GRILL
DRIVE-THRU

Guava Cheesecake

Pollo Tropical® is one of the most popular quick-service restaurant concepts. Our chicken is fresh, never frozen, and is free of hormones and trans-fats. Our menu started with a simple recipe for citrus-marinated chicken grilled on an open flame and has grown to offer a variety that is unsurpassed. The company also licenses the concept at Florida International University, University of Florida and Florida State University.

1½ C. chocolate-wafer or graham-cracker crumbs
½ C. (1 stick) butter, melted
2 tbsp. plus 2 C. sugar
1 C. guava paste
½ C. fresh lemon juice
2 lb. cream cheese, at room temperature
4 extra-large eggs
2 tsp. vanilla extract
1 tbsp. grated lemon zest
¼ C. guava marmalade or red currant jelly

1. Heat oven to 350°F (175°C). Butter a 9-inch springform pan. Mix crumbs, butter and 2 tablespoons sugar; press over the bottom and up the side of the pan. Bake until almost dry, about 10 minutes. Set aside. (Leave oven on.)

2. Heat guava paste and lemon juice in a saucepan over medium heat, whisking, until melted. Set aside.

3. Beat the cream cheese and 2 cups sugar with an electric mixer until light and fluffy. Beat in eggs, one at a time, then vanilla, lemon zest and melted guava paste. Pour into crust.

4. Wrap aluminum foil around the bottom and sides of springform pan and place in a large roasting pan. Add 1 inch boiling water. Bake until the top is firm and the filling no longer jiggles when shaken, about 90 minutes. Turn off the heat, open the oven door a few inches, and let the cheesecake cool 20 minutes before transferring to a cooling rack. Cover and refrigerate cooled cheesecake at least 6 hours.

5. Thirty minutes before serving, melt jelly with 1 tablespoon water, whisking, and gently brush on top. Chill at least 30 minutes more before serving.

320 Southeast 1st Street, Miami, FL

Pollo Tropical

"Music with dinner is an insult both to the cook and the violinist."
G.K. Chesterton

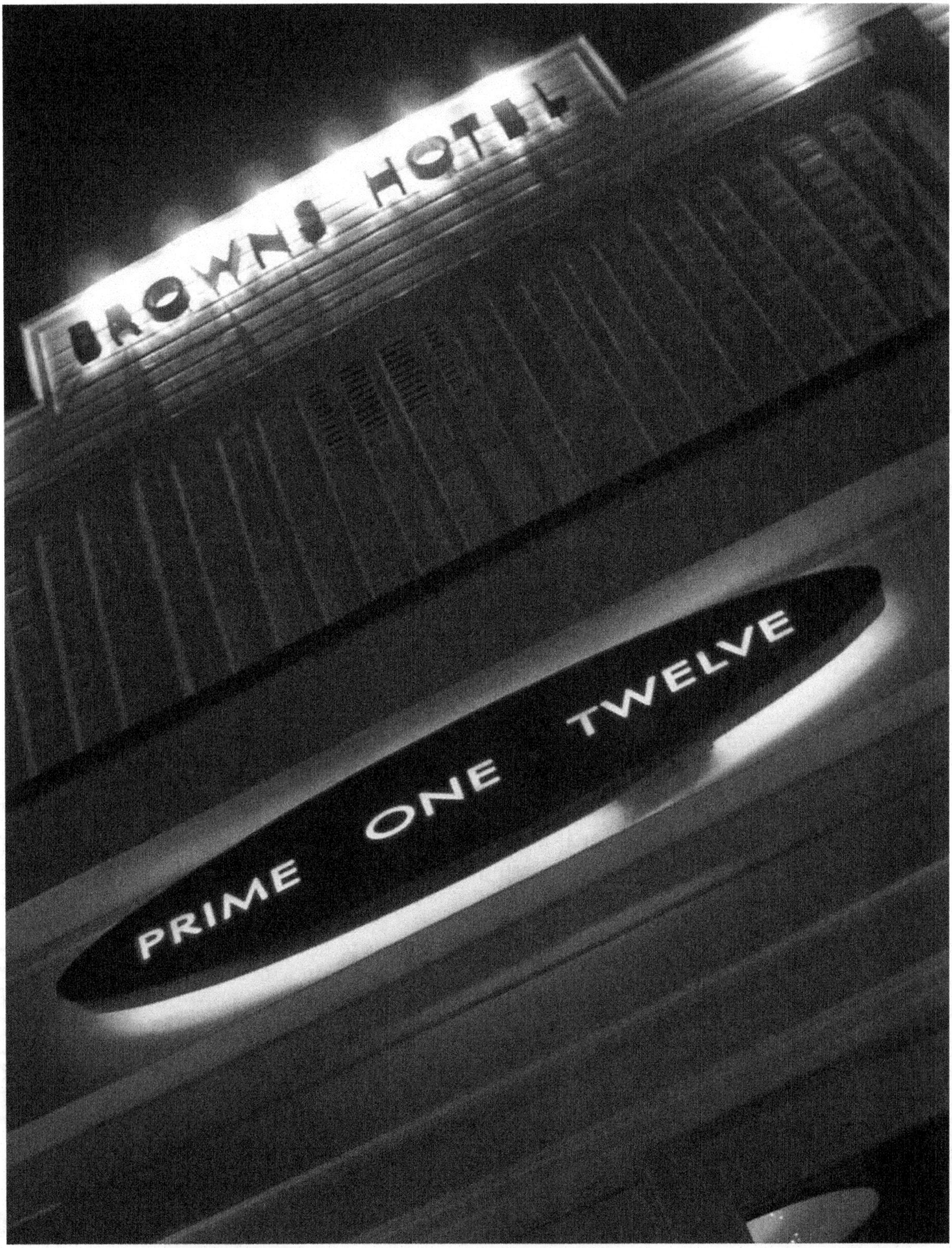
BROWNS HOTEL
PRIME ONE TWELVE

Fried Oreos with French Vanilla Ice Cream

Prime 112 is a positively excellent steakhouse and it's just a shame you can't get a table—at least not without a reservation as much as a week in advance during the season. Ah, but once you are seated in this trendy restaurant in the SoFI section of South Beach, you're in for a treat. Go with the Sauteed Hudson Valley Foie Gras, Organic Field Greens, and 48 ounce Porterhouse for Two, with six sauces, five butters, and eleven accessories to choose from. And while you're waiting for your meal, enjoy the enticing eye-candy that frequents this hot new area of South Beach.

Fried Oreos:
2 quarts vegetable oil for frying
1 large egg
1 C. milk
2 tsp. vegetable oil
1 C. pancake mix
1 (18 oz.) package cream-filled chocolate sandwich cookies

French Vanilla Ice Cream:
8 large eggs
3 C. sugar
8 C. whipping cream
4 C. milk
8 tsp. vanilla extract

Fried Oreos:
1. Heat oil in deep-fryer to 375 degrees F (190 degrees C).
2. Whisk together the egg, milk, and 2 teaspoons of vegetable oil in a bowl until smooth. Stir in the pancake mix until no dry lumps remain. Dip the cookies into the batter one at a time, and carefully place into the hot frying oil.
3. Fry only 4 or 5 at a time to avoid overcrowding the deep fryer. Cook until the cookies are golden-brown, about 2 minutes. Drain on a paper towel-lined plate before serving.

French Vanilla Ice Cream:
1. Whisk the eggs in a mixing bowl until light and fluffy, 1 to 2 minutes.
2. Pour in the sugar, a little at a time, then continue whisking until completely blended, about 1 minute more.
3. Pour in the cream, milk, and vanilla and whisk to blend.
4. Transfer the mixture to an ice cream maker and freeze following the manufacturer's instructions.

Prime 112 Restaurant
112 Ocean Drive, Miami Beach, FL

"You can tell a lot about a fellow's character by his way of eating jellybeans."
Ronald Reagan

Lyonnaise Salad

vAt Provence Grill, classic French Bistro fare is prepared using authentic recipes and only the freshest and finest ingredients. We have brought on award winning Chef,Roly Cruz-Taura as a consultant to create this cozy eatery with friendly staff and exceptional cuisine, nestled at the west end of Lincoln Road, far enough away from the hustle and bustle of South Beach living. One taste of chef de cuisine Christopher Szyjka's daily creations and you will feel that you have been transported to a French countryside inn or a Paris street cafe.

½ lb. frisée (French curly endive)
6 oz. slab bacon or thick-cut bacon slices
2 tbsp. distilled white vinegar
4 large eggs
2 tbsp. chopped shallot
3 tbsp. red-wine vinegar

1. Tear frisée into bite-size pieces and put in a large bowl. If using slab bacon, cut lengthwise into ¼-inch-thick slices. Cut bacon slices crosswise into ¼-inch-thick sticks (lardons).

2. In a heavy skillet cook bacon over moderate heat, stirring occasionally, until golden and remove skillet from heat.

3. Have ready another skillet with 1 inch warm water. Half-fill a 4-quart saucepan with water and stir in white vinegar.

4. Bring liquid to a bare simmer. Break each egg into a teacup. Slide 1 egg into simmering liquid and immediately push white around yolk with a slotted spoon, moving egg gently. (Egg will become oval, with yolk completely covered by white.) Add remaining 3 eggs in same manner.

5. Simmer eggs about 1 ½ minutes for runny yolks to about 3 minutes for firm yolks. (Serving this salad with runny—not fully cooked—yolks may be of concern if there is a problem with salmonella in your area.) Immediately transfer eggs to skillet of warm water.

6. Reheat bacon in its skillet over moderate heat. Add shallot and cook, stirring, 1 minute. Add red-wine vinegar and boil 5 seconds. Immediately pour hot dressing over frisée and toss with salt and pepper to taste.

7. Divide salad among 4 plates and top with drained poached eggs. Season eggs with salt and pepper and serve salad immediately.

1223 Lincoln Road, Miami Beach, FL

Provence Grill

"Tofu tacos are not Mexican. I think putting tofu on anything and calling it Mexican is an insult to my people."
Simone Elkeles

Fried Snapper

Signature Taste of MIAMI

Pubbelly is the collaborated creation of Andreas Schreiner, Jose Mendin & Sergio Navarro. These 3 young entrepreneurs and hospitality professionals have joined forces to make their dream a reality, creating the first Asian inspired Gastropub in Miami. Located in the western part of Miami Beach, this tavern like restaurant will feature true gastropub fare such as homemade pate's, duck and pork rillettes, specialty terrines, braised dishes, homemade sausages and pickled vegetables along with it's signature and innovative haute Asian street food.

⅓ C. (55g) raisins
2 tbsp. verjuice (see note) or boiling water
1 tbsp. chopped thyme leaves
Grated zest and juice of ½ lemon
1 ½ tbsp. extra virgin olive oil
4 x 180g red snapper fillets, pin-boned
olive oil spray
½ tsp. honey
1 bunch flat-leaf parsley, leaves picked
¼ C. (40g) toasted pine nuts
50g reduced-fat feta, crumbled

1. Soak raisins in verjuice for 5 minutes until softened slightly. Drain, reserving liquid.

2. Meanwhile, combine thyme, zest and 2 tsp oil in a bowl. Season to taste and mix well to combine. Rub all over fish.

3. Heat a large frypan over medium heat and spray lightly with the olive oil spray. In batches if necessary, cook fish skin-side down, for 5 minutes or until golden. Turn the fish and cook for a further 2 minutes until cooked through. Transfer to a plate, cover loosely with foil and keep warm.

4. Whisk lemon juice, honey, remaining oil and reserved raisin liquid together in a bowl. Season to taste, then add the parsley, pine nuts, crumbled feta and soaked raisins and toss to combine.

5. Serve the fish with the parsley salad.

1418 20th Street, Miami Beach, FL

Pubbelly

"Whoever thought a tiny candy bar should be called fun size was a moron."
Glenn Beck

Salmon with Andouille Sausage and Crab Stuffing

6 ea 5-6 oz Salmon fillets
1½ Tbsp. seafood seasoning
non-stick cooking spray, fat-free

Stuffing:
1 sleeve Ritz crackers, crushed
6 oz. Andouille sausage, diced small
1 C. (8 oz) lump crab meat
¼ C. butter, melted
1½ tsp. parsley, dried
1 ea. green onion, chopped
4 oz. Monterey Jack cheese, shredded

Sauce:
10 oz. container prepared Alfredo sauce
½ tsp. seafood seasoning
4 oz. Monterey Jack cheese, shredded
½ C. parmesan cheese, grated
¼ C. Chablis wine
¼ C. half and hal

1. Preheat the oven to 400 degrees.

2. Spray a 9x13 baking dish with Nonstick Cooking Spray. Use a knife to cut a large pocket in the side of each piece of fish. Place in 9x13 pan and set aside.

3. To make the sausage and crab stuffing, mix all the stuffing ingredients in a large mixing bowl, stir until well combined.

4. Place ½ cup stuffing in each piece of fish and flatten the fish slightly so it cooks more evenly

5. Lightly spray the fish with non-stick cooking spray and sprinkle with Seafood Seasoning. Carefully add ¼ cup water around the fish, not poured over the fish.

6. Place in oven and cook 20-25 minutes or when the stuffing reaches 140-150 degrees.

Red Lobster
13300 Biscayne Boulevard, North Miami, FL

"If you're afraid of butter, use cream."
Julia Child

Molten Chocolate Cake

Located in Miami Beach's South of Fifth neighborhood, Red boasts modern noir décor that incorporates Miami's spicy flair. Featuring only the finest Certified Angus Beef Prime on and off the bone, Red's menu – created by Executive Chef, Peter Vauthy – is a hybrid of classic cuisine and the freshest seasonal ingredients. Everything from the sauces to garnishes is prepared from scratch – sure to convert even the staunchest of vegetarians into ravenous carnivores.

Signature Tastes of MIAMI

4 tbsp. unsalted butter, room temperature, plus more for muffin tins
⅓ C. granulated sugar, plus more for muffin tins
3 large eggs
⅓ C. all-purpose flour
¼ tsp. salt
8 oz. bittersweet chocolate, melted
Confectioners' sugar, for dusting
Whipped Cream, for serving

1. Preheat oven to 400 degrees. Generously butter 6 cups of a standard muffin tin. Dust with granulated sugar, and tap out excess. Set aside.

2. In the bowl of an electric mixer fitted with the paddle attachment, cream the butter and granulated sugar until fluffy. Add eggs one at a time, beating well after each addition. With the mixer on low speed, beat in flour and salt until just combined. Beat in chocolate until just combined. Divide batter evenly among prepared muffin cups.

3. Place muffin tin on a baking sheet; bake just until tops of the cakes no longer jiggle when the pan is lightly shaken, 8 to 10 minutes. Remove from oven; let stand 10 minutes.

4. To serve, turn out cakes, and place on serving plates, bottom sides up. Dust with confectioners' sugar, and serve with whipped cream, if desired.

Red The Steakhouse
119 Washington Avenue, Miami Beach, FL

"Books allow you to take flight, unlike the chicken wings I stapled to my back before eating them. "
Jarod Kintz

Homemade Pasta

Signature Tastes of MIAMI

From the heart of Milano to the center of Miami, twin brother Chefs Roberto and Emanuele Bearzi bring their unique talents and passion for authentic Cucina Italiana to RISTORANTE FRATELLI MILANO, offering a genuine taste of home. With over 30 years combined experience in some of the top kitchens in town, Roberto works his magic as Chef de Cuisine while Pastry Chef Emanuele fills the air with the scents of homemade pasta, freshly baked bread and confections to delight the most discerning diners. Joined by Roberto's charming wife Fiorella, RISTORANTE FRATELLI MILANO welcomes you!

*500g 00 plain flour
(see note)
5 large eggs
2 tbs extra virgin
olive oil
1 tsp salt*

1. Place the flour on a clean work surface and make a well in the centre. Crack the eggs into the well and add the oil and salt.

2. Use your fingers to whisk the eggs and gradually bring in the flour from the sides. Continue stirring and kneading until flour is incorporated. Knead on a lightly floured surface for 10 minutes or until dough is smooth and elastic.

3. Cover with plastic wrap and set aside for 30 minutes to rest.

Ristorante Fratelli Milano
213 Southeast 1st Street, Miami, FL

"To make my meal in a box taste better, I decided to tweak the logo, rather than the ingredients."
Jarod Kintz

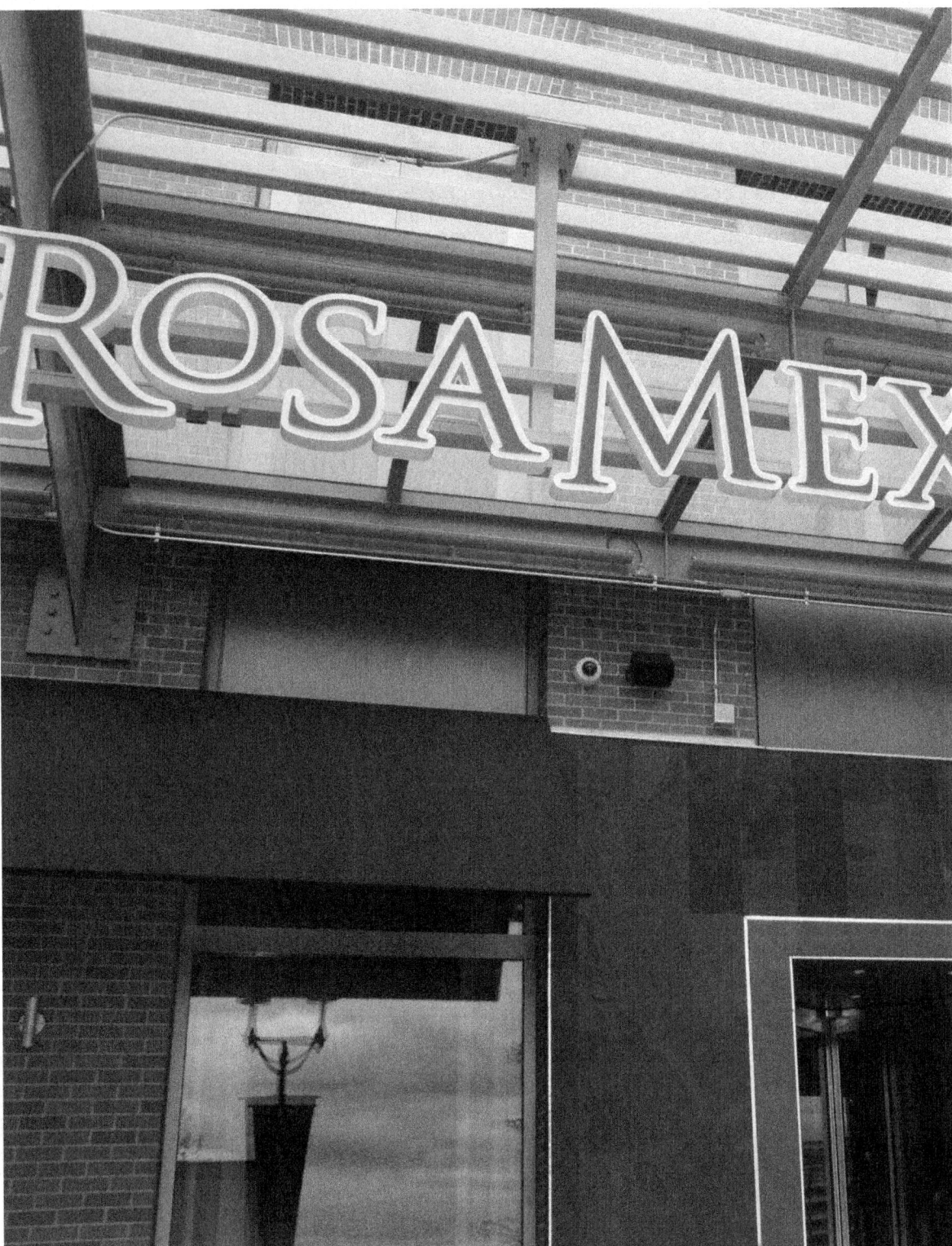

Espresso Flan

When we opened the first Rosa Mexicano in 1984, New York Magazine applauded us for introducing New Yorkers to a "hitherto unfamiliar, elevated version of Mexican cuisine." Today, we continue to redefine expectations nationwide with our authentic Mexican cooking, stylish spaces and festive atmosphere. All of our award-winning dishes remain faithful to their traditional roots while incorporating regional accents and inspired innovation. You'll know just what we're talking about when you try our Pomegranate Margaritas or Guacamole en Molcajete, made in a traditional lava-rock mortar and prepared tableside.

5 eggs
2 egg yolks
1 C. sugar
1 tsp. vanilla extract
1¼ C. heavy cream
1 C. whole milk
1 C. caramel
Pinch grey salt
1 stick (½ C.) melted butter
6 tbsp. hot brewed espresso

Caramel:
½ C. water
1 C. sugar

1. In a large bowl, whisk together egg and egg yolks. While whisking add the sugar slowly until fully dissolved. Add vanilla, heavy cream, milk, and salt and continue to whisk. In order to get rid of air bubbles in mixture, transfer to large bowl through a fine strainer.

2. In the bottom of 6 (½ cup) ramekins (small ceramic custard cups), place about 1½ teaspoons of caramel. When all 6 ramekins have caramel at the bottom, brush each bottom and side with melted butter to secure flan and yet allow it to be removed easily.

3. Fill each ramekin with the flan mixture, SLOWLY to avoid air bubbles, until about ⅔ full.

4. Preheat the oven to 350 degrees F.

5. Place almost full ramekins in shallow baking pan and then fill the pan with boiling water. The hot water bath will allow the flan cups to cook evenly in the oven. Right before placing pan in oven, top each ramekin with a tablespoon of hot espresso. Bake for 40 minutes.

6. When removing pan from oven, allow the ramekins to remain cooling in their original water bath, overnight if necessary.

Rosa Mexicano
900 South Miami Avenue, Miami, FL

"I have made a lot of mistakes falling in love, and regretted most of them, but never the potatoes that went with them."
Nora Ephron

Gorgonzola Pizza

Signature Tastes of MIAMI

Rosinella is owned and operated by Mamma Rosinella, Papa Antonio and their children: Paolo, Roberto, Tonino, Luciano Rosanna. Mamma was born in a small town in the south of Italy called Palazzo San Gervaso. Papa came from a neighboring town called Bella. They got married and moved to Rome where they started their family. On April 23, 1993 they opened their first restaurant, Sport Café at 534 Washington Avenue. On February 23, 1997, Rosinella on Lincolin Road opened. One year later on March 23, 1998, Mamma opened in downtown Miami in Brickell Village.

1 loaf (1 lb.) frozen bread dough, thawed
2 tbsp. butter
2 tbsp. brown sugar
2 large sweet onions, thinly sliced and separated into rings
3 tbsp. olive oil
2 tsp. dried basil
2 tsp. dried oregano
1 tsp. garlic powder
2 plum tomatoes, chopped
1 C. (4 oz.) shredded part-skim mozzarella cheese
3 oz. crumbled Gorgonzola or blue cheese
2 tbsp. grated Parmesan cheese
¼ C. pitted Greek olives, chopped

1. Divide bread dough in half. Press each portion onto a 12-in. pizza pan coated with cooking spray; build up edges slightly. Prick dough several times with a fork. Cover and let rise in a warm place for 30 minutes.

2. Meanwhile, in a large skillet over medium heat, melt butter with brown sugar. Add onions; cook for 20-30 minutes or until golden brown, stirring occasionally.

3. Brush dough with oil. Combine the basil, oregano and garlic powder; sprinkle over dough. Bake at 425° for 10 minutes.

4. Arrange onions and tomatoes over crusts; sprinkle with cheeses and olives. Bake 8-10 minutes longer or until golden brown.

Rosinella

1040 South Miami Avenue, Miami, FL

"Training is everything. The peach was once a bitter almond; cauliflower is nothing but cabbage with a college education."
Mark Twain

Fried Chicken Wonton

This place is in a super shady-looking shopping plaza on 107th and NW 7th Street. It's actually a great and affordable restaurant! It's really great for lunch. The food itself was delicious- really authentic. If you like the taste of homemade authentic food, you will love this place. It's also a great price for the big portions you get.

6 sheets rolls pati
½ C. chicken mince
½ tsp. salt
3 green onion
half cabbage
garlic as required
oil for fry
1 egg
½ C. all purpose flour

For Dip Sauce:
1 Tbsp. garlic
3 Tbsp. oil
½ C. oyster sauce
1 Tbsp. sugar
1½ C. water
1½ Tbsp. corn flour
1 pinch salt

1. Heat oil in the pan and fry garlic.

2. Then add chicken and fry for five minutes on high flame.

3. Then add salt, cabbage and onion and cook further for 2 to 3 minutes.

4. Now put flour and egg in bowl and mix well to form a sticky paste.

5. Then apply paste on the edges of roll sheets.

6. Now fill chicken wonton mixture in the roll sheets and seal extracting all the air out.

7. Now deep fry the wontons.

8. Tasty fried chicken wonton is ready to serve.

For Dip Sauce:
1. Heat oil in the pan and fry garlic.

2. Now add oyster sauce, salt, sugar and water and boil for three minutes.

3. Then add corn flour and simmer it till thick.

4. Pour in a serving bowl, sauce is ready.

Royal Thai Restaurant
10648 Fontainebleau Boulevard, Miami, FL

"When the food runs out, the family reunion is over. It's cool that out of all my relatives, I'm the only cannibal."
Jarod Kintz

Roasted Asparagus

One of the most authentic and exciting restaurants to open in Miami Beach in ages, this ultra-friendly restaurant has made fast friends of the neighborhood around Sunset Harbor. The young, mostly Italian staff is exceptionally knowledgeable and helpful. Highlights on the lengthy menu of rustic dishes include spaghetti bottarga, orecchiette with wild boar sausage and nearly melted broccoli di rabe pesto. Salt-crusted branzino, prepared in the wood-burning ovendeboned table-side, is a masterpiece.

1 lb. asparagus spears (thick spears are best for roasting)
1-2 tbsp. olive oil
2 cloves garlic, minced
kosher salt
freshly grated black pepper
lemon juice

1. Preheat oven to 400°F. Rinse clean the asparagus. Break the tough ends off of the asparagus and discard.

2. Lay the asparagus spears out in a single layer in a baking dish or a foil-covered roasting pan. Drizzle olive oil over the spears, roll the asparagus back and forth until they are all covered with a thin layer of olive oil. (Alternatively you can put the asparagus and oil in a plastic bag, and rub the bag so that the oil gets evenly distributed.) Sprinkle with minced garlic, salt, and pepper.

3. Rub over the asparagus so that they are evenly distributed.

4. Place pan in oven and cook for approximately 8-10 minutes, depending on how thick your asparagus spears are, until lightly browned and tender when pierced with a fork. Drizzle with a little fresh lemon juice before serving.

Sardinia Ristorante
1801 Purdy Avenue, Miami Beach, FL

"Life is half delicious yogurt, half crap, and your job is to keep the plastic spoon in the yogurt."
Scott Adams

Broccoli Rabe

Victoria Pesce Elliott, Food Critic, Miami Herald.- Scott Conant, formerly of L'Impero and Alto, is at the helm of Scarpetta™, Fontainebleau Miami Beach's Italian restaurant and an outpost of his recently opened restaurant of the same name in New York City. The restaurant features ocean and poolside views, a wraparound veranda as well as casual dining areas and a cocktail lounge. Scarpetta regional menu comprises clean, crisp flavors prepared in layers to reflect the quality of locally sourced ingredients. Known for coaxing the most sublime flavors out of the simplest ingredients, Conant relies on Florida's bounty of farm-fresh and organic produce to craft menus of surprising complexity.

4 bunches (12 to 16 oz. each) broccoli rabe (rapini), stems trimmed
¼ C. olive oil
3 garlic cloves, chopped
½ tsp. dried crushed red pepper flakes
⅓ C. raisins
Salt
2 tbsp. pine nuts, toasted

1. Working in batches, cook the broccoli rabe in a large pot of boiling salted water until crisp tender, about 1 minute per bunch. Transfer the broccoli rabe to a large bowl of ice water to cool.

2. Reserve about ¼ cup of the cooking liquid. Strain the cooled broccoli rabe and set aside.

3. Heat the oil in a heavy large skillet over medium heat. Add the garlic and red pepper flakes, and saute until the garlic is golden, about 1 minute. Reduce heat to medium-low.

4. Add the broccoli rabe and toss to coat. Add the reserved cooking water, the raisins, and cook until the broccoli rabe is heated through and the stems are tender, about 4 minutes. Season with salt, to taste. Just before serving, toss the mixture with the pine nuts.

4441 Collins Avenue, Miami Beach, FL

Scarpetta

"The first time you see something that you have never seen before, you almost always know right away if you should eat it or run away from it."
Scott Adams

Beef Tataki

Shibui Japanese restaurant opened its doors in 1981. This a family owned and operaterd restaurant. We have received a number of awards over these years. Shibui not only keeps its traditional japanese cuisine but is also moving along with the availability of ingredients from all over the world and creating fusion style dishes for for example the japeruvian ceviche which has been a hit in our business. We have also been the original creators of few rolls that you can actually find all over Miami, like the Luisiana, Caliente, and Margy rolls.

For the Beef:
2 lb. whole, trimmed beef tenderloin (filet), chilled
1 Tbsp. vegetable oil
2 Tbsp. sweet soy sauce (optional, available at Asian markets)
¼ tsp. freshly ground black pepper
⅓ C. low-sodium soy sauce
¼ C. mirin (sweet Japanese cooking wine) or sherry
3 green onions, white and light green parts only, thinly sliced
2 large cloves garlic, thinly sliced
zest of 1 lemon, removed in strips with a vegetable peeler

For the Ponzu Sauce:
4 Tbsp. low-sodium soy sauce
2 Tbsp. rice vinegar
1½ Tbsp. turbinado, raw, or brown sugar
1 Tbsp. fresh lemon juice
1 Tbsp. fresh lime juice
1 tsp. ginger juice (see Note)
2 Tbsp. very finely snipped fresh chives

1. Preheat the oven to 500 degrees F. Be sure to let it reach its temperature before roasting the beef.

2. Rub all sides of the beef with the vegetable oil, then rub in the soy sauce, if using, and season with the pepper.

3. Place on a rack over a roasting pan and sear in the hot oven for 15 minutes. The internal temperature, in the very center, should be 115 degrees F. Immediately transfer the roasting rack to a tray (to catch the juices; do not keep over the roasting pan or the beef will continue to cook).

4. Set in a cool place to stop the cooking as quickly as possible. In a heavy-duty resealable plastic bag large enough to hold the beef, combine the soy sauce, mirin, green onions, garlic, and lemon zest. As soon as the beef is cool enough to handle, transfer to the bag and refrigerate for at least 6 hours and up to 24 hours, turning over occasionally.

"The thought of two thousand people crunching celery at the same time horrified me."
George Bernard Shaw

Key Lime Pie

Mr. E.L. "Shorty" Allen left Georgia as a young man more than 60 years ago. In 1951 he built and opened the familiar log cabin style restaurant, including family size picnic tables, screen windows and a concrete floor. Since those early days, Shorty's has been satisfying appetites with our famous ribs, chicken, homemade sauce, creamy cole slaw, and of course our delicious corn on the cob.

For Crust:
1¼ C. graham cracker crumbs from 9 (2¼ in. by 4¾-in.) crackers
2 Tbsp. sugar
5 Tbsp. unsalted butter, melted

For Filling:
1 (14-oz) can sweetened condensed milk
4 large egg yolks
½ C. plus 2 Tbsp. fresh or bottled key lime juice (if using bottled, preferably Manhattan brand)

For Topping:
¾ C. chilled heavy cream

Make Crust:
1. Preheat oven to 350°F.
2. Stir together graham cracker crumbs, sugar, and butter in a bowl with a fork until combined well, then press mixture evenly onto bottom and up side of a 9-inch (4-cup) glass pie plate.
3. Bake crust in middle of oven 10 minutes and cool in pie plate on a rack. Leave oven on.

Make Filling and Bake Pie:
1. Whisk together condensed milk and yolks in a bowl until combined well. Add juice and whisk until combined well (mixture will thicken slightly).
2. Pour filling into crust and bake in middle of oven 15 minutes. Cool pie completely on rack (filling will set as it cools), then chill, covered, at least 8 hours.

Make Topping:
1. Just before serving, beat cream in a bowl with an electric mixer until it just holds stiff peaks. Serve pie topped with cream.

Shorty's Bar-B-Q 40th
11575 Southwest 40th Street, Miami, FL

"I like a cook who smiles out loud when he tastes his own work. Let God worry about your modesty; I want to see your enthusiasm."
Robert Farrar Capon

Corn Nuggets

Sparky's Roadside Barbecue opened a year ago in downtown Miami. Owners Hans Seitz (from Queens, New York), and Kevin Kehoe (from Woodbury, Long Island). Do it they did, and Sparky's has been packing its 48 seats on NE Second Avenue and First Street ever since. The storefront restaurant exudes a down-home, roadside coffee-shop ambiance, with wooden tables painted in pastel green and a roll of paper towels upon each one (as of now there is no air-conditioning, but plenty of whirling fans).

1 (11 oz.) can creamed corn
1 (11 oz.) can whole kernel corn, drained
½ C. yellow cornmeal
½ C. all-purpose flour
1 egg white
2 tbsp. milk
salt and pepper to taste
3 C. vegetable oil for deep frying

1. In a medium bowl, stir together the creamed corn and drained whole kernel corn. Line a baking sheet with aluminum foil, and coat with vegetable oil or cooking spray. Drop spoonfuls of the corn mixture onto the sheet, and freeze until firm, about 3 hours.

2. Heat one inch of oil to 350 degrees F (175 degrees C) in a large deep skillet, or fill a deep-fryer with oil as directed by the manufacturer.

3. Mix together the cornmeal, flour, egg white, milk, salt and pepper in a medium bowl. Dip frozen corn nuggets in the batter, and quickly fry in hot oil until golden brown. Remove to paper towels to drain.

Sparky's Roadside Barbecue
204 Northeast 1st Street, Miami, FL

"He showed the words "chocolate cake" to a group of Americans and recorded their word associations. "Guilt" was the top response. If that strikes you as unexceptional, consider the response of French eaters to the same prompt: "celebration."
Michael Pollan

Ravioli di Ricotta

Located in the Heart of the Art Deco District of Miami Beach, in front of the Impala Hotel, For over 13 years, Spiga Restaurant has been offering an intimate atmosphere, with a romantic and poetic decoration, along with the quality and simplicity of its food. At Spiga we keep the same staff since the beginning, and that's the reason why our costumers are treated by their names and why the waiters know their preferences.

For the filling:
1 lb. fresh spinach
1 lb. ricotta cheese, thoroughly drained
1 egg
4 oz. parmigiano reggiano cheese, freshly grated
salt and pepper
pinch of nutmeg

For the dough:
3 C. flour
4 eggs
1 tbsp. extra-virgin olive oil

For the dressing:
4 oz. unsalted butter
10 fresh sage leaves
4 oz. freshly grated parmigiano cheese

1. Boil the spinach in lightly salted water. Place the boiled spinach in a cheese cloth and form a small sack. Squeeze the sack to expel as much water as possible. Chop the spinach finely.

2. Place the spinach in a bowl. Combine the drained ricotta, egg, parmigiano cheese, salt, pepper, and a generous pinch of nutmeg. Taste and adjust the salt, pepper, and nutmeg if necessary.

3. Prepare the pasta dough using the recipe for fresh pasta. Make the dough very soft and moist. Use the minimum flour necessary, just enough to prevent the dough from sticking to your hands while working. Cut the dough in two parts. Place one of the pieces on the work surface, and flatten it with a rolling pin until it is very thin.

4. Repeat the same steps with the other half of the dough, making a pasta sheet of the same size. Set it aside, covered with a moist towel if necessary to prevent the pasta from drying too much.

5. Place about 1 teaspoon of the filling on the dough, spaced 2 inches (5 cm) apart.

6. In a skillet large enough to contain the ravioli, place the butter and sage leaves. Turn the heat on just long enough to melt the butter. Bring water to a boil in a stockpot. Gently drop the ravioli in the boiling water a few at a time.

7. Cook until the pasta is al dente (firm but not too soft or overcooked). Drain ravioli, picking them from the boiling water with a slotted spoon.

8. Transfer the ravioli to the pan. Stir gently until they are evenly coated with the butter. Combine the grated cheese. Place in a warm serving dish and serve at once.

SPIGA Ristorante Italiano
1228 Collins Avenue, Miami Beach, FL

"I don't know what it is about food your mother makes for you, especially when it's something that anyone can make - pancakes, meat loaf, tuna salad - but it carries a certain taste of memory."
Mitch Albom

SPRIS
PIZZA PASTA E VINO
of CORAL GABLES
DINNER
www.spriscoralgables.com

Pizza Margherita

Spris (pronounced "sprees") is named after the famous aperitif from the Veneto Region. Our logo tells only part of the story: a gentle cloud of rising bubbles indicates a bubbly mix of Italian sparkling wine called Prosecco, Aperol (an Italian specialty aperitif similar to Campari) and a splash of soda water. Spris is a casual spot on South Beach's blossoming Lincoln Road - good for a quick bite while the rest of the world skates by. Pizzas are the main draw, where over 30 tantalizing varieties of Spris' famed thin-crusted pizza are delicately baked in a wood-burning brick oven.

Pizza Dough:
2 tsp. instant yeast
1 ½ C. warm water (100°F to 115°F)
2 tbsp. honey
3½ - 3¾ C. King Arthur 100% Organic White Whole Wheat Flour
1 tbsp. vital wheat gluten
1½ tsp. salt
2 tbsp. extra-virgin olive oil
2 tbsp. sesame seeds

Toppings:
3 tbsp. extra-virgin olive oil
4 ripe plum tomatoes, sliced into thin rounds
2 C. diced fresh mozzarella cheese
12 fresh basil leaves
½ tsp. bread salt or other fine salt

1. Preheat the oven to 425°F. If you're using a baking stone, preheat the oven to 450°F.

To Make the Dough:
1. Stir together the yeast, water, honey, and 1 cup of the flour in a large mixing bowl, in the bowl of a stand mixer, or in the bucket of a bread machine. Cover the mixture and let it stand for 30 minutes; it'll be very soupy.
2. Add 2 cups of the remaining flour, the vital wheat gluten, and the salt to the yeast mixture, along with the olive oil and sesame seeds. Mix and knead the dough-by hand, mixer, or bread machine-for about 5 minutes, adding more flour as necessary to make a smooth elastic dough.
3. Place it in a lightly greased bowl, cover the bowl tightly with plastic wrap, and allow the dough to rise for at least 2 hours, or until it's doubled in size.

Assembling the Pizza:
1. Divide the dough in half, roll each piece on a floured surface into a 13" to 15" round (depending on the size of your pizza pans), and place the rounds on lightly oiled pans. (A 13" diameter yields a thin crust; a 15" diameter yields a cracker-thin crust.) Turn in the overhanging edge to form a rim.
2. If you plan to use a baking stone to bake the pizza, place the dough on two baker's peels, dusted with cornmeal or surfaced with parchment.
3. Brush each round with 1 tablespoon of the olive oil. Divide the tomato slices between the rounds. Divide the cheese and sprinkle it on top of the tomatoes. Divide the basil leaves and sprinkle them on top of the cheese. Divide and sprinkle on the salt and the remaining 1 tablespoon of oil.
4. Bake the pizzas in the pans for 20 to 30 minutes, or until the top and bottom crusts are nicely browned. If you're using baking stones, bake for 15 to 25 minutes (leaving the pizza on the parchment), or until the crust is nicely browned on the bottom.
5. Cut into wedges and serve immediately, garnished with additional fresh basil, if desired.

731 Lincoln Road, Miami Beach, FL

Spris

"There's no better feeling in the world than a warm pizza box on your lap."
Kevin James

Toasted Bagel

SUSHISAMBA swung open its doors on Park Avenue South in New York City in 1999. Since then, we've celebrated over 10 years of singular, soulful style and superlative dining, proudly opening six locations, including a second in New York City, as well as one in Miami Beach, Chicago, Las Vegas (in The Shoppes at The Palazzo) and London (opening this July!). London is our first international location, which will occupy the 38th and 39th floors of the City's newest skyscraper: Heron Tower.

4 to 6 oz. Buddig (or any brand) dried beef slices
4 oz. cream cheese, softened
1 C. real mayonnaise (do not use Miracle Whip salad dressing - too sweet)
1 C. sour cream
½ sweet onion, diced very finely
2 tsp. dill weed
2 tbsp. dried parsley flakes
¼ tsp. celery salt
¼ tsp. garlic powder
¼ tsp. onion powder
8 plain bagels, halved and toasted, then each half cut into 8 wedges

1. Dice dried beef quite finely.
2. Cream together softened cream cheese and mayonnaise.
3. Stir in sour cream and onion.
4. Stir in seasonings, mixing together well.
5. Cover and chill several hours before serving.
6. Just before serving, toast bagel halves and cut into wedges. You can do this ahead of time and keep them in a covered container, but they WILL lose their crispness if you do this. I really like the crunchiness, so I try to wait until serving time to toast them, but it won't affect the taste at all if you want to toast them ahead of time...whatever is your preference and works for your schedule!
7. To serve, place beef spread in a bowl in the center of a large platter and surround the bowl with the toasted bagel wedges.

Sushi Samba Dromo
600 Lincoln Road Miami Beach, FL

"To set but a low value upon toast is to expose one's deficiencies in right appreciation."
E.V. Lucas, 'When Toasters Disagree' (1906)

SUSHI SIAM
JAPANESE & THAI

Mussels Dynamite

The cuisine at Sushi Siam consists of many combinations and blends of different flavors, herbs and spices. It is fiery cuisine which has become very popular. The Sushi and Thai foods are prepared fresh daily. Our variety of fresh ingredients offers the most nutritious and wholesome ways to enjoy your meal. At Sushi Siam we work hard to bring you the finest of our cuisine.

8 New Zealand green mussels in the shell, rinsed and drained
2 sticks chopped imitation crab
4 tbsp. masago (Smelt Egg)
3 tbsp. chili garlic sauce
1 tsp. sesame oil
4 oz. enoki mushrooms
½ C. Dynamite(R) Sauce
¼ C. tsume sweet sauce (eel sauce)
4 tablespoons thinly sliced green onions
salt and pepper

1. Preheat oven to 450 degrees F
2. Blanch mussels (still in shell) in boiling water for 2 min and drain.
3. Extract mussels from their shells. Rinse and drain well using your hands to squeeze as much excess water from mussels.
4. Reserve shells and scrub thoroughly.
5. Cut each mussel into small pieces (about 4-6 pieces each)
6. Prepare the filling by mixing, in a mixing bowl, mussels, imitation crab, ½ of the masago, ½ of the chili garlic sauce, and sesame oil.
7. Spread the enoki mushrooms over the insides of the shells.
8. Layer the filling over the mushrooms and arrange on a foil-lined baking sheet.
9. Bake for 7-10 minutes then remove from oven.
10. Top with the rest of the dynamite sauce and broil until the surface is golden brown (about 2-3 minutes).
11. Top with Tsume sweet sauce, masago, and green onions immediately before serving.
12. Alternate Serving Idea: This dish can also be prepared and served as a plate. Instead of cooking individually, place all ingredients on one serving medium such as an oven-proof plate. An inverted portabella mushroom with the stem removed works excellent as well!

931 Brickell Avenue, Miami, FL

Sushi Siam

"Mussels may be invisible to most folks, including anglers. But if you don't protect them they're gone, and with them a critical link in the whole chain of natural resources."
Dan Tredinnick

Aji Amarillo

Come and explore the diversity of our sushi and ceviche... Submerge your taste buds in an explosion of flavors offered in this culinary fusion. Let us make you a delicious meal, healthy for your body. Suviche brings you a combination never seen before that fuses Japanese and Peruvian cuisine. Suviche's vision is to focus on a light, healthy, fresh meal delivered promptly while very affordable. Suviche will lead a new generation of people seeking healthier lifestyles.

2 tbsp. aji amarillo paste (or one aji amarillo pepper, chopped and sauteed in oil)
½ C. mayonnaise
¼ C. sour cream
1 tbsp. ketchup
2 green onions, white and green parts, chopped
juice of 1-2 limes (to taste)
salt and pepper to taste

1. Coarsely chop the white parts of the green onions.

2. Add the chopped onions with all the rest of the ingredients (except the salt and pepper) to the bowl of a food processor or blender.

3. Process until mixture is smooth and creamy.

4. Season sauce with salt and pepper to taste, and chill until ready to serve.

49 Southwest 11th Street, Miami, FL

SuViche

"If more of us valued food and cheer above hoarded gold, it would be a much merrier world."
J.R.R. Tolkien

Pollo Asado

For the best in Tex-Mex takeout, come to Taco Rico where you can mix it up with a Tex Mex Chop bowl or spice it up with jalapeno poppers. We also offer mind-blowing combinations of enchiladas, fajitas, burritos, tacos and quesadillas. All of our menu items are served with tasty steak, chicken, pork, or beans and loaded with toppings like melted cheese, sour cream and pico de gallo. If you also want dessert, try some of our fried ice cream or homemade flan.

½ C. olive oil
1 tsp. ground cumin
1½ tsp. salt
1 tsp. dried oregano
2 tbsp. garlic, minced
⅓ C. lime juice
⅓ C. orange juice
½ tsp. achiote powder
4 whole boneless chicken breasts, skin attached

1. Cut chicken breasts into two halves. Heat oil in small saucepan over medium high heat until very hot. While oil heats, mash cumin, salt, oregano, garlic and achiote powder into a paste with a mortar and pestle.

2. Place the paste in a heat-proof bowl. Whisk hot oil into the garlic paste. Allow to cool slightly then add lime and orange juice, stirring well to combine. Pour marinade into a large zi-ploc bag, add chicken breast halves.

3. Shake or knead to spread marinade through-out chicken. Refrigerate at least four hours to overnight. Grill over medium heat, turning, until chicken reaches internal temperature of 180 de-grees.

4. Place chicken on cutting board and let rest several minutes.

5. Serve individually, or cut into bite sized pieces for making tacos or burritos.

Taco Rico Tex-Mex Café
1608 Alton Road, Miami Beach, FL

"I am a better person when I have less on my plate."
Elizabeth Gilbert, Eat, Pray, Love

Ensalada Rusa

Signature Tastes of MIAMI

Tapas are not necessarily a particular kind of food; rather, they represent a style of eating, and a way of life that is so very Spanish and yet so adaptable in America. Tapas are as varied as the cooks who create them and in Spain range from the simplest fare, like grilled chorizo sausage, flavorful jamón Serrano (cured ham), Manchego cheese, and simple canapés, to surprisingly sophisticated dishes using caviar, fresh snails and baby eels. They can be foods we traditionally eat as appetizers, but more often than not cross the line into what we might think of as first course or main course dishes. Tapas are usually served in small portions and they are meant for immediate gratification.

1 or 2 large potatoes
100g (4oz) young green beans
2 eggs
tin of tuna
green or black olives, pitted (some chopped)
mayonnaise (home-made or Mr Hellman's!)
salt and freshly-ground black pepper
sqeeze of fresh lemon juice

1. Peel the potatoes and cut into small dice of about 1cm. Boil in salted water for about 10 mins or until soft. Drain and leave to cool.

2. Hard boil the eggs then remove the shells and leave in cold water to cool. When they're cool enough to handle, chop into cubes and place in a bowl with the potato.

3. Blanch the beans and refresh in cold water to retain their 'bite'. Then add these and the chopped olives to the bowl. Finally, add the tuna, the mayonnaise, the salt and pepper and the lemon juice and mix gently to combine.

4. Garnish with the whole olives, maybe some flat-leaf parsley and serve.

5. There are many variations on this dish. Some have carrots, or peas, or capers, or anchovies, or red pepper (capsicum), or mustard - or a combination of all the above!

6. Try it all and see what suits you best.

Tapas & Tintos
448 Espanola Way, Miami Beach, FL

"Part of the secret of success in life is to eat what you like and let the food fight it out inside."
Mark Twain

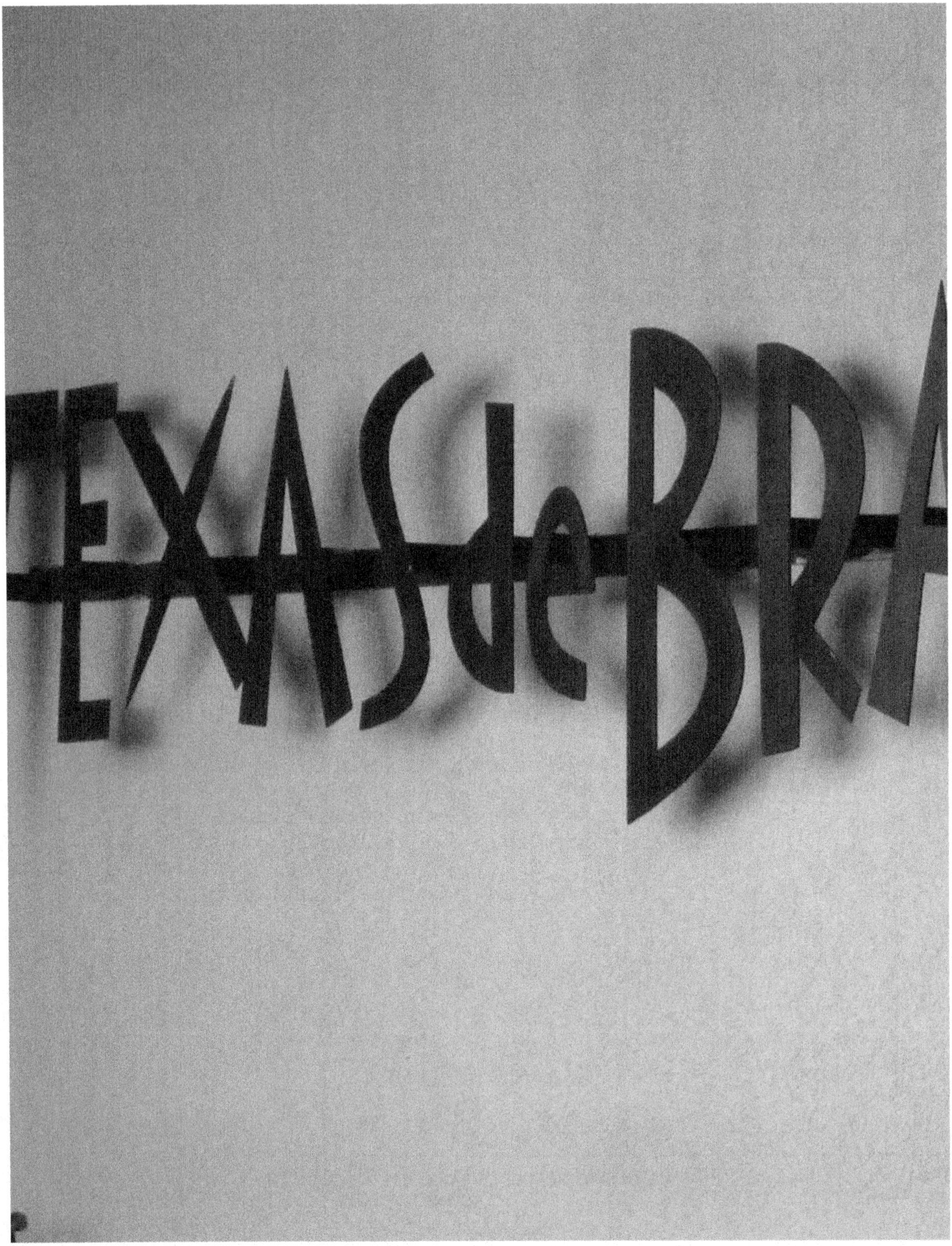
TEXAS de BRA

Grape Salad with Gorgonzola Cheese

Signature Tastes of MIAMI

It's a regular occurrence at Texas de Brazil, the newest addition to a quickly growing field of churrascarias, or Brazilian steakhouses. This suburban Dallas-based restaurant chain follows the now well-known formula: Start with a massive salad bar and then let the meat fest begin. Every diner has a small coaster-sized disk. When it's green, the waiters — dressed as gauchos from the Pampas — come by the tables offering various cuts of meats. They keep coming until the diner flips the disk to show red. Stop.

1½ C. red seedless grapes
1½ C. green seedless grapes
1½ C. mayonnaise
1 Tbsp. lemon juice
¾ C. crumbled gorgonzola cheese

1. Combine all ingredients in a large bowl.

2. Mix well.

3. Refrigerate before serving.

Texas De Brazil
300 Alton Road, Miami Beach, FL

"Vulgarity is the garlic in the salad of life."
Cyril Connolly

Tofu Salad

All our food is prepared to order. It is delicious and best of all it is very healthy. We take great pride in preparing out Thai dishes which makes each dish a work of art. We hope you feel comfortable in our Thai atmosphere. If this is your first experience with Thai cuisine, we are certain that it will not be your last. Finally, Thai House South Beach was opened to meet the demands of our loyal customers. We are proud to serve you with spectacular food and outstanding service.

250 gms tofu
50 gms green beans
50 gms carrots
1 tbsp. oyster sauce
1 tbsp. light soy sauce
1 tbsp. oil
3 red-green chillies
1 garlic clove
1 tsp. lime juice
1 tbsp. fish sauce
(Use pinch of salt for vegetarian)
½ tsp. sugar
1 tbsp. chopped celery
sliced cherry tomatoes
sliced cucumber

1. Chop the carrots and green beans until fine. Fry with the oyster sauce, light soy sauce, and oil for a few minutes. Spoon into the middle of the plate.

2. Surround with slices of cucumber and cherry tomatoes.

3. Blend the chillies and garlic together, add the chopped celery, fish sauce, lime juice, and sugar and blend more. This is the sauce.

4. Cut the tofu into pieces and deep fry to give it a crunchiness, cut into strips and pile ontop of the green beans in the plate.

5. Just before serving, spoon the spicy sauce over the top of the dish.

1137 Washington Avenue, Miami Beach, FL

Thai House

"Tofu tacos are not Mexican. I think putting tofu on anything and calling it Mexican is an insult to my people."
Simone Elkeles, Rules of Attraction

Shrimp Cocktail

Our impressive menu of nationally renowned dry aged steaks and the freshest of seafood will ignite your culinary imagination as our award-winning wine list of more than 5,000 bottles awakens your inner sommelier. And as our gracious, knowledgeable servers delight you with their uncanny ability to anticipate your every need, you'll experience firsthand why the American Culinary Federation recently bestowed upon us their "Achievement of Excellence Award."

32 shell-on (21 to 25 count) tiger shrimp

For the Brine:
¼ C. kosher salt
¼ C. sugar
1 C. water
2 C. ice

For the Cocktail Sauce:
1 (14½ oz) can diced tomatoes, drained
½ C. prepared chili sauce
4 Tbsp. prepared horseradish
1 tsp. sugar
few grinds fresh black pepper
½ tsp. kosher salt
1 Tbsp. olive oil
sprinkle Old Bay seasoning

1. Using a pair of scissors or a serrated knife, make an incision down the backside of the shrimp, following the intestinal track. Eviscerate shrimp and rinse under cool water leaving shells intact.

2. Place cleaned shrimp into a bowl with brine and refrigerate mixture for 20 to 25 minutes. While shrimp are brining, place tomatoes, chili sauce, horseradish, sugar, pepper, and salt in food processor and blend until smooth. Refrigerate cocktail sauce until ready to serve.

3. Place a baking sheet or broiler pan under oven broiler and preheat for 5 minutes. Remove shrimp from brine and drain thoroughly. Rinse the shrimp under cold water and dry on paper towels. In a large bowl, toss shrimp with olive oil and sprinkle with Old Bay seasoning, if desired.

4. Place shrimp onto a sizzling sheet pan and return to broiler immediately. After 2 minutes, turn the shrimp with a pair of tongs. Return the shrimp to broiler for 1 minute. Transfer to a cold cookie sheet. Refrigerate immediately.

5. Once shrimp have chilled, arrange with cocktail sauce in a martini glass or as desired.

The Capital Grille
444 Brickell Ave., Miami, FL

"I shall be but a shrimp of an author."
Thomas Gray

Lamb Meatballs

Signature Tastes of MIAMI

The Dining Room is an intimate restaurant, on Washington Ave, south of Fifth. This hidden gem features small plates made with locally sourced, sustainable ingredients, an eclectic wine list and seasonal beer selection. Chef Horacio Rivadero, Executive Chef of OLA Restaurant, reflects his commitment to locally grown ingredients in the restaurant's menu; which often varies, taking advantage of that which is freshest in the market that day.

1 tbsp. unsalted butter
5 shallots, minced
2 lb. ground lamb
1 C. fresh bread crumbs
¼ C. chopped fresh parsley
1 egg, lightly beaten
2 tbsp. lemon zest
½ tsp. dried marjoram
salt and freshly ground black pepper to taste
½ C. unsalted butter
1 tbsp. olive oil
2 ½ tbsp. tomato sauce
¼ C. wine
1 small garlic clove, minced
1 dash ground cinnamon
toothpicks

1. Melt the 1 tablespoon butter in a skillet over medium heat. Cook and stir the shallots in the skillet until tender. Transfer to a large bowl.

2. Mix lamb, bread crumbs, parsley, egg, and lemon zest into the bowl with the shallots. Season with marjoram, salt, and pepper. Let stand 1 hour in the refrigerator.

3. Melt ½ cup butter and heat olive oil in a skillet over medium-high heat. Form the lamb mixture into small meatballs, and cook in the skillet in batches until evenly brown. Do not drain skillet. Drain meatballs on paper towels, and place in a serving dish.

4. Mix tomato sauce, wine, garlic, and cinnamon into the skillet. Cook and stir until well blended and heated through. Drizzle over the meatballs in the dish. Serve with toothpicks.

413 Washington Avenue, Miami Beach, FL

The Dining Room

"I don't know what it is about food your mother makes for you, especially when it's something that anyone can make - pancakes, meat loaf, tuna salad - but it carries a certain taste of memory."
Mitch Albom

Chili Cheese Taters

Signature Tastes of MIAMI

10 potatoes, peeled and sliced
½ C. flour
2 tsp. seasoning salt
½ tsp. pepper
2 (15 oz.) cans chili
2 C. skim milk
1 lb. cheese Velveeta cheese, cubed

1. Mix flour, seasoning salt, and pepper together.

2. Place ½ of sliced potatoes on the bottom of the crock pot. Then sprinkle ½ the flour mixture over the potatoes. Next is 1 can of chili on top.

3. The rest of the potatoes go on top the chili. The last of the flour mix. Then the last can of chili. And finally pour the milk over all.

4. Cook on low for 6-8 hours or high for 3 hours. ½ hour before it is finished, add the cheese and stir.

5. After cheese is melted, it is ready to eat.

The Filling Station
95 Southeast 2nd Street, Miami, FL

"Age is not important unless you're a cheese."
Helen Hayes

the forge
RESTAURANT WINEBAR · SHAREEFMALNIK

Apple Pie Sundae

Signature Tastes of MIAMI

Apple Pie:
4 lg. fuji apples sliced thin
¼ C. sugar
¼ C. light brown sugar
¾ tsp. ground cinnamon
¾ C. all-purpose flour
6 tbsp. butter
hagen daz vanilla ice cream

Butter Rum Sauce:
1 C. sugar
½ C. butter
½ C. heavy cream or half and half
1 tsp. rum extract
1 tsp. vanilla

1. Preheat oven to 400 degrees. Spray A 9 X 13 inch pan with cooking spray just to coat pan. Arrange apple slices in pan.
2. Mix together ¼ cup white sugar, ¼ cup brown sugar and the cinnamon. Sprinkle over the apple slices. Mix 1/3 cup white sugar with the flour.
3. Cut in the butter until crumbly. Spoon mixture over apples.
4. Bake at 400 degrees for 35 to 40 minutes, or until done. Let cool 20 minutes.

To Make the Butter Rum Sauce:
1. In a medium sauce pan combine the sugar, butter, and cream. Using medium to low heat, heat the sugar, butter and cream until the butter melts and the sugar dissolves.
2. Add the rum extract and vanilla and stir until mixed in.

To Assemble:
1. Place a serving of apple mixture in a bowl or goblet, top the apple mixture with 1 scoop of vanilla ice cream. Drizzle the caramel sauce over the ice cream.

432 41st Street, Miami Beach, FL

The Forge

"If you wish to make an apple pie from scratch, you must first invent the universe."
Carl Sagan

The Warren family has owned and operated The Frieze since 1993. Since that time, our owners, Lisa and Robert worked tirelessly to achieve one primary objective for the company: maintaining product quality above all else. The Frieze and the Warren family has a new, and even more challenging goal – to spread The Frieze's exceptional product far and wide and educate people about truly great ice cream and sorbet! Lisa and Robert are thrilled to have their son, David, take the lead on this challenge as he learns the ups and downs of business and ice cream.

5 oz. sweetened condensed milk
1 tsp. vanilla extract
2 C. powdered sugar
14 oz. Premium shredded coconut or flaked coconut
24 oz. milk chocolate chips
1 C. whole dry roasted almonds

1. Blend the condensed milk and vanilla. Add the powdered sugar to the above mixture a little at a time, stirring until smooth. Stir in the coconut. The mixture should be firm. Pat the mixture firmly into a greased 9x13x2-inch pan.

2. Chill in the refrigerator until firm. In a double boiler over hot, not boiling water, melt the chocolate, stirring often. You may also use a microwave. Remove the coconut mixture from the refrigerator and cut it into 1x2-inch bars.

3. Put 2 whole almonds atop each bar. Set each coconut bar onto a fork and dip it into the chocolate. Tap the fork against the side of the pan or bowl to remove any excess chocolate. Air dry at room temperature on waxed paper for several hours.

4. You may speed up the process by putting in the refrigerator for 30 minutes.

The Frieze Ice Cream Factory
1626 N Michigan Ave, Miami Beach, FL

"A fit, healthy body—that is the best fashion statement"
Jess C. Scott

Caprese Salad

At The Oceanaire Seafood Room, our commitment to freshness sets us apart from the rest. Only top-of-the-catch fish from the world's most reputable suppliers is served, and each dish is carefully crafted to ensure the restaurant's high standards of quality and flavor are exceeded. The menu is based on market availability, therefore our selections change each day.

2 C. balsamic vinegar
3 whole ripe toma-
toes, sliced thick
12 oz. weight
mozzarella cheese,
sliced thick
fresh basil leaves
olive oil, for drizzling
kosher salt and
freshly ground black
pepper

1. In a small saucepan, bring balsamic vinegar to a boil over medium-low heat. Cook for 10 to 20 inutes, or until balsamic has reduced to a thicker glaze. Remove from heat and transfer to a bowl or cruet. Allow to cool.

2. When you're ready to serve, arrange tomato and mozzarella slices on a platter. Arrange basil leaves between the slices. Drizzle olive oil over the top of the salad, getting a little bit on each slice. Do the same with the balsamic reduction, making designs if you want. Store extra balsamic reduction in fridge for a later use.

3. End with a sprinkling of kosher salt and black pepper. Serve as a lunch, with crusty bread. Or serve alongside a beef main course for dinner.

The Oceanaire Seafood Room
900 South Miami Avenue, Miami, FL

"Salad is never more appetizing than when served in a large wooden bowl."
Dorothy Draper

255

Calamari Salad

Since 2003, The River Seafood & Oyster Bar has been serving the freshest available local, sustainable and organic cuisine; resulting in a fare that is a modern twist on classic seafood. The River, and Executive Chef David Bracha, pride themselves on a unique menu designed with attention to detail ensuring superior quality. The River's sleek, yet comfortable, dining room is as perfect for a special dinner for two as it is for a celebration with friends.

Signature Tastes of MIAMI

1 ½ lb. cleaned squid
2 tbsp. fresh lemon juice
1 tbsp. red-wine vinegar
⅓ C. extra-virgin olive oil
1 large garlic clove, minced
½ tsp. salt
¼ tsp. black pepper
1 small red onion, halved lengthwise, then thinly sliced crosswise (1 C.)
⅓ C. pitted Kalamata olives, halved lengthwise
2 C. cherry or grape tomatoes (¾ lb), halved or quartered if large
2 celery ribs, cut into ¼-inch-thick slices
1 C. loosely packed fresh flat-leaf parsley leaves

1. Rinse squid under cold running water, then lightly pat dry between paper towels. Halve tentacles lengthwise and cut bodies (including flaps, if attached) crosswise into 1/3-inch-wide rings.

2. Cook squid in a 5- to 6-quart pot of boiling salted water , uncovered, until just opaque, 40 to 60 seconds. Drain in a colander and immediately transfer to a bowl of ice and cold water to stop cooking. When squid is cool, drain and pat dry.

3. Whisk together lemon juice, vinegar, oil, garlic, salt, and pepper in a small bowl, then stir in onion and let stand 5 minutes.

4. Meanwhile, combine squid, olives, tomatoes, celery, and parsley in a large bowl. Toss with dressing and season with salt and pepper. Let stand at least 15 minutes to allow flavors to develop.

The River Seafood and Oyster Bar
650 South Miami Avenue, Miami, FL

"You don't win friends with salad."
Homer Simpson

257

Roasted Beets with
White Balsamic and Goat Cheese

Located in the heart of Florida's Riviera, Sunny Isles Beach, Timo has become an icon of neighborhood restaurants since opening in 2003. With Chef Tim Andriola's Italian-Mediterranean inspired cuisine, attentive seamless service and a timeless, contemporary dining room, Timo has earned a following of South Florida and national pundits equally. The restaurant's warm inviting atmosphere is the perfect place for a quick bite, an intimate meal, or a fun meeting place to gather with family and friends.

2 beets (scrubbed)
1 bunch mache (lamb s lettuce rinsed and dried)
1 bunch arugula (rinsed and dried)
2 peaches (fresh, peeled pitted and sliced)
2 shallots (chopped)
¼ C. pistachio nuts (chopped)
4 oz goat cheese (crumbled)
¼ C. walnut oil
2 Tbsp. balsamic vinegar
salt
pepper

1. Preheat oven to 375 degrees F (190 degrees C). Wrap each beet in two layers of aluminum foil, and place onto a baking sheet. Bake in the preheated oven until the beets are tender, about 1 hour and 20 minutes. Allow the beets to cool slightly, then remove the skins. Let the beets cool to room temperature, or refrigerate until cold. Once cooled, thinly slice the beets.

2. Place the mache and arugula into a large mixing bowl. Add the sliced beets and peaches; sprinkle with the shallots, pistachios, and goat cheese. In a separate bowl, whisk together the walnut oil, balsamic vinegar, salt, and pepper until emulsified, and pour over the salad mixture. Toss well, and serve.

17624 Collins Avenue, Sunny Isles Beach, FL

Timo

"A good cook is like a sorceress who dispenses happiness."
Elsa Schiaparelli

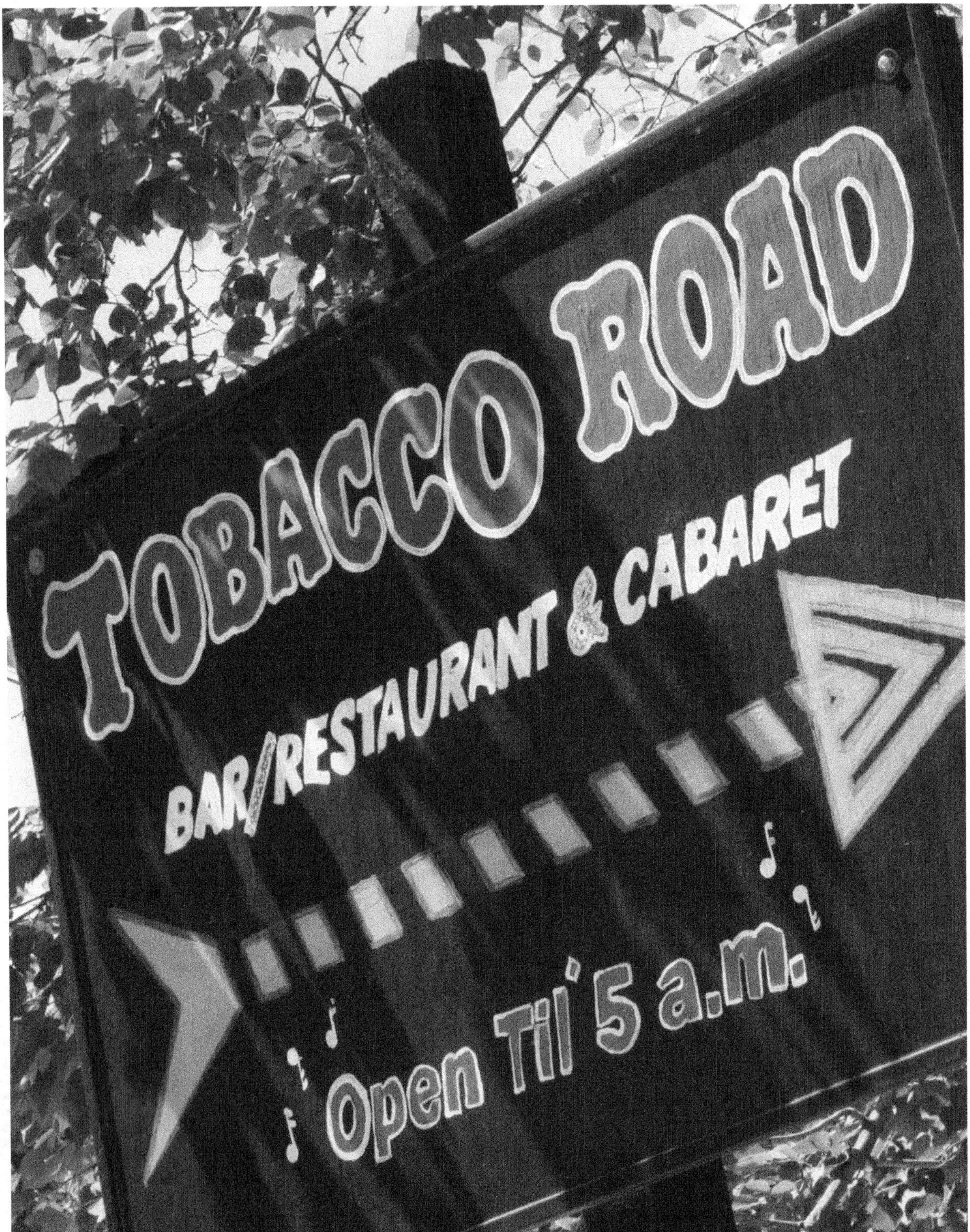
TOBACCO ROAD
BAR/RESTAURANT & CABARET
Open Til' 5 a.m.

Roast Beef Club

An old-time favorite, Tobacco Road was established in 1912 and has a somewhat shady history of run-ins with local law enforcement authorities. That said, it's the absolute best place in town to find a huge greasy hamburger and you're liable to hear some of the best live blues music in the country while you're dining. The menu includes typical bar fare, including a great greasy cheeseburger. If you're looking for a healthy meal, The Road is definitely not the place to go. However, if you're looking for a great burger and a beer at a decent price, you'll love this joint.

1 lb. Certified Angus Beef ® deli roast beef, thinly sliced
1 French baguette, cut into four equal servings and sliced in half
2 tsp. olive oil
4 oz. blue cheese
¼ C. finely chopped fresh chives
Mayonnaise
12 slices precooked bacon
1 tomato, thinly sliced
½ red onion, thinly sliced
fresh ground black pepper to taste

1. Preheat oven to 350ºF. Brush French bread with olive oil and toast cut side up. Remove from oven and cool slightly, spread blue cheese on one half of each sandwich. Add chopped chives and fresh ground pepper. Spread mayonnaise on remaining slices.

2. Assemble, arrange 4 ounces of roast beef on blue cheese side of sandwich. Top with bacon, tomato and red onion.

3. Slice each sandwich in half and serve with seasonal fresh fruit or your favorite salad.

Tobacco Road
626 South Miami Avenue Miami, FL

"Carnal embrace is the practice of throwing one's arms around a side of beef."
Tom Stoppard, Arcadia

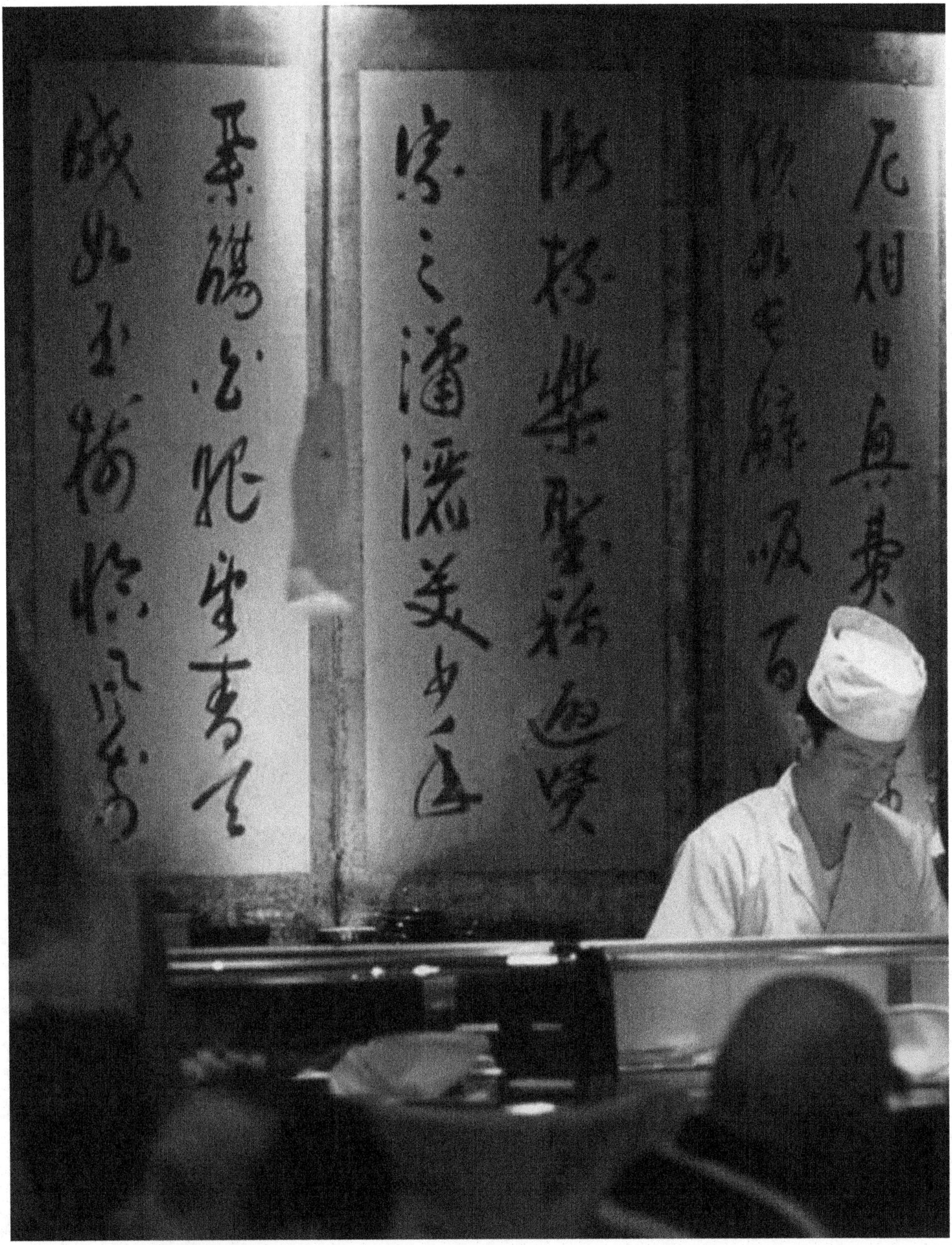

Shrimp Scampi with Pasta

Established in 1987, Toni's Sushi Bar is the first Japanese restaurant in Miami Beach. Through the years, we have remained committed to serving only the freshest and most authentic sushi. As the second oldest restaurant in South Beach, we are celebrating our 25th year in business and invite you to enjoy the best sushi Miami has to offer. - Toni

½ lb. pasta
2 tbsp. butter
2 tbsp. extra virigin olive oil
½ large shallot, finely diced
3 cloves garlic, sliced
Pinch of red pepper flakes
½ lb. shrimp, peeled
Salt and pepper
¼ C. dry white wine
juice of half a lemon
handful of parsley, chopped

1. Bring a large pot of water to a boil. And a couple tablespoons of salt, then add the pasta. Cook according to the instructions on the pasta box. Drain when done.

2. Meanwhile, drop one tablespoon of the oil and one tablespoon of the butter into a large skillet. Melt the butter of medium-high heat. Add the shallots, garlic, and red pepper flakes. Cook until the shallots are translucent, about 2-3 minutes.

3. Add the shrimp and cook for about 3 minutes, turning halfway through. Remove the shrimp when pink, and set aside. Add the wine and lemon juice to the skillet, and bring to a boil. Add the rest of the butter and oil. Stir the sauce

4. Return the shrimp to the skillet, season with salt and pepper, then add the drained pasta. Toss to combine everything. Add a little pasta water if the mixture is too dry. Serve with a sprinkle of parsley.

1208 Washington Avenue, Miami Beach, FL

Toni's Sushi

"Tis an ill cook that cannot lick his own fingers."
William Shakespeare

Filet Mignon

We invite you to escape to Truluck's. A getaway for the senses. Come savor the freshest Crab, direct from our own fisheries. Delight in our fresh-catch seafood menu or select tender, juicy steaks prepared to perfection. Then complement it all with delicious wines by the glass and bottle.

Truluck's Restaurant
777 Brickell Avenue, Miami, FL

3 Tbsp. unsalted butter
1 lb. mixed wild mushrooms, such as shiitake and cremini, trimmed
kosher salt and freshly ground pepper
4 (6-oz) beef fillets, about 1½ in. thick
1 shallot, finely chopped
2 Tbsp. grainy mustard
1 C. heavy cream
2 Tbsp. chopped fresh flat-leaf parsley, plus more for garnish, optional

1. Heat 2 tablespoons butter in a large, heavy nonstick skillet over medium-high heat until hot. Add the mushrooms and ½ teaspoon salt and ½ teaspoon pepper. Cook, stirring occasionally, until browned, about 6 minutes.

2. Wipe out the skillet. Heat the remaining 1 tablespoon butter in the skillet over high heat until hot. Sprinkle the beef generously with salt and pepper. Sear over medium-high heat, turning once halfway through, until browned, about 12 minutes for medium. Transfer the beef to a platter.

3. Add the shallots to the skillet and cook over medium heat, stirring, until golden, about 3 minutes. Add the mustard and heavy cream and bring to a boil, cooking until slightly thickened, about 3 minutes. Stir in the parsley. Spoon the sauce on a plate; place the beef on the sauce and scatter the mushrooms over top. Garnish with additional parsley, if desired.

"I hate people who are not serious about meals. It is so shallow of them."
Oscar Wilde

Heirloom Tomato Soup

Tudor House, presided over by Chef Geoffrey Zakarian - the renowned culinary name behind New York hot spots The Lambs Club and The National, cookbook author and top Food Network personality - occupies the ground floor corner space of the Dream South Beach Hotel and what was once the Tudor Hotel, keeping reverence for the building's history and simultaneously reinventing it. The restaurant's light, airy décor combines a unique perspective on modern design with accessibility that feels utterly Miami.

Good tasting extra virgin olive oil
3 medium onions, chopped
salt and freshly ground black pepper
4 large cloves garlic, minced
Pinch hot red pepper flakes
1 generous tbsp. tomato paste
2½ to 3 C. chicken broth (homemade preferred, but low sodium canned works, too)
a big handful fresh basil leaves, torn
15 medium or 10 large delicious ripe tomatoes, cored and coarsely chopped (do capture their juices for the soup)
1 C. heavy cream (for serving)

1. Generously film the bottom of a 12-quart pot with olive oil. Set over medium high heat. When warm, add onions and about ¼ teaspoon each salt and pepper. Cook, stirring occasionally, until onions start to color.

2. Stir in the garlic, red pepper, and tomato paste. Cook 1 minute. Add broth, basil, and tomatoes. Bring to a lively simmer, cover the pot, and cook 15 to 20 minutes, or until tomatoes are softened and soup tastes fresh, but mellow. Adjust seasonings to taste.

3. Once soup has cooled, puree two-thirds in a blender or food processor. Rewarm or serve close to room temperature. The all-important finish is stirring a generous tablespoon of cream into each bowl.

Tudor House
1111 Collins Avenue, Miami Beach, FL

"Only the pure in heart can make a good soup."
Ludwig van Beethoven

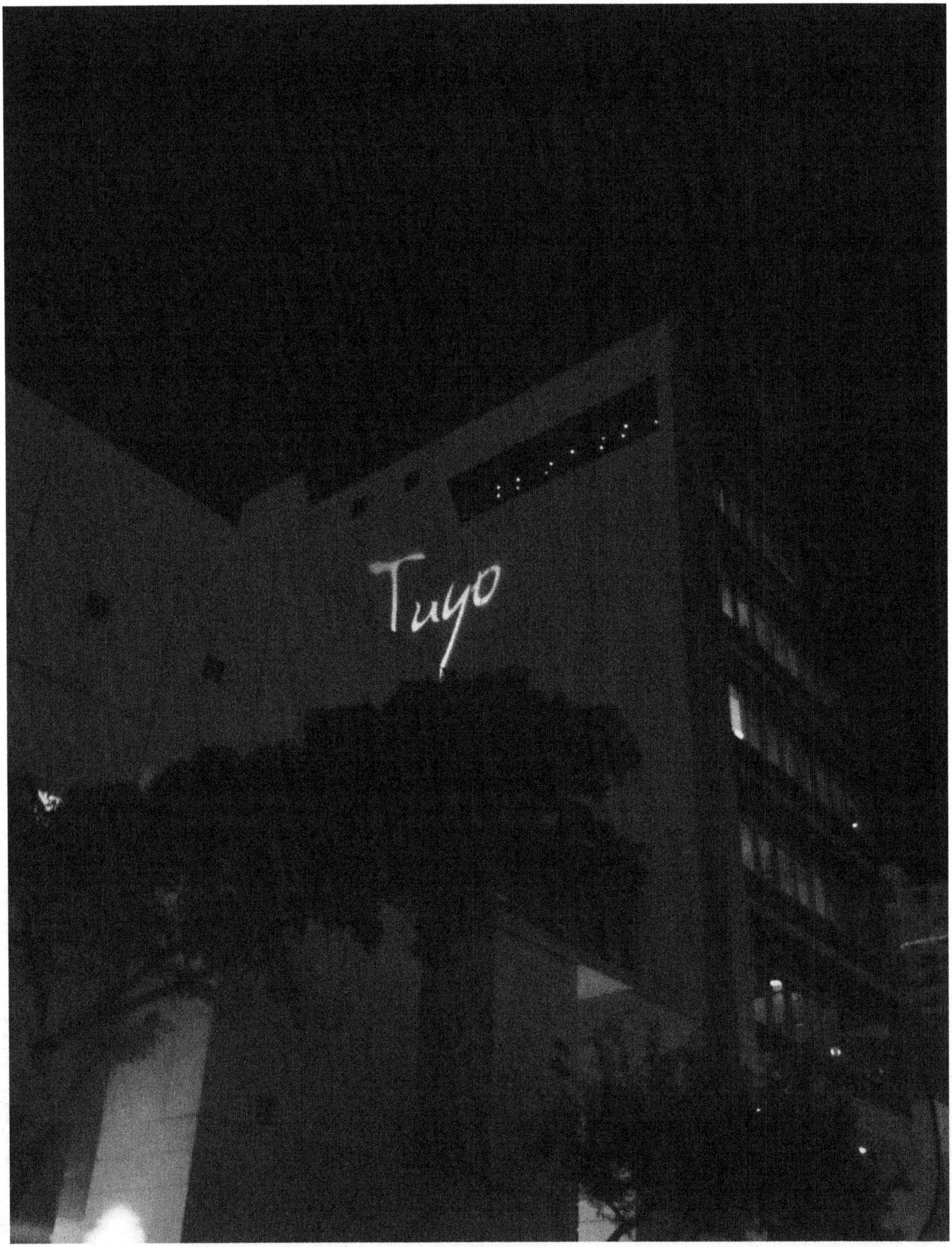
Tuyo

Molten Chocolate Cake

Tuyo is the crown jewel sitting atop Miami Dade College's new Miami Culinary Institute, offering a spectacular view of the bay and Miami skyline. Its breakthrough recipe for culinary excellence in the 21st century infuses a trailblazing menu with the Institute's state-of-the-art approach to the culinary arts, setting the table for food culture innovation by focusing on environmentally sound practices and drawing upon the food grown locally and in the Institute's edible organic garden.

*1 stick (4 oz) unsalted butter
6 oz bittersweet chocolate, preferably Valrhona
2 eggs
2 egg yolks
¼ C. sugar
pinch of salt
2 Tbsp. all-purpose flour*

1. Preheat the oven to 450°. Butter and lightly flour four 6-ounce ramekins. Tap out the excess flour. Set the ramekins on a baking sheet.

2. In a double boiler, over simmering water, melt the butter with the chocolate. In a medium bowl, beat the eggs with the egg yolks, sugar and salt at high speed until thickened and pale.

3. Whisk the chocolate until smooth. Quickly fold it into the egg mixture along with the flour. Spoon the batter into the prepared ramekins and bake for 12 minutes, or until the sides of the cakes are firm but the centers are soft. Let the cakes cool in the ramekins for 1 minute, then cover each with an inverted dessert plate. Carefully turn each one over, let stand for 10 seconds and then unmold. Serve immediately.

MAKE AHEAD: The batter can be refrigerated for several hours; bring to room temperature before baking.

Tuyo Restaurant
415 Northeast 2nd Avenue, Miami, FL

"Let's face it, a nice creamy chocolate cake does a lot for a lot of people; it does for me."
Audrey Hepburn

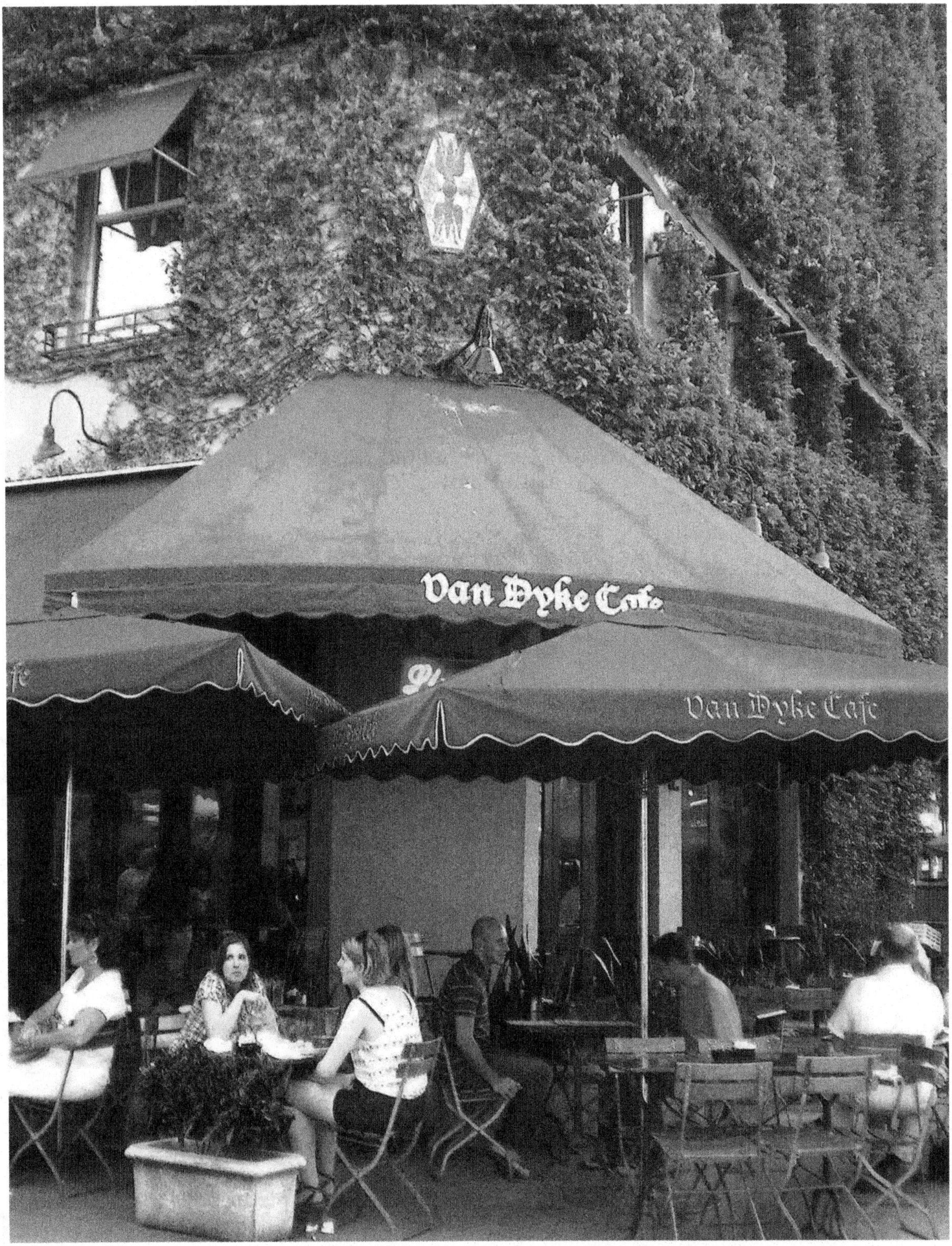
Van Dyke Cafe
Van Dyke Cafe

Penne Al Salmone

After nearly two decades, the Van Dyke Café's continued success can be attributed to the fare as well as its staff's even-keeled and generous personalities. The European-style indoor-outdoor café housed in the historic Van Dyke building, with its signature red awnings, has always been known for its wide ranging menu. In fact, the Van Dyke remains one of the few places on Lincoln Road to enjoy breakfast anytime, given that the café is open daily from 8 AM until 2 AM on the weekends and genres from fun and latin to soul and R&B, in addition to jazz. The live music begins nightly at 9 PM.

1 salmon fillet
1 C. whipping cream
2 C. tomato sauce
1 C. of white sliced mushrooms
1 fluid oz. vodka
2 tbsp. of minced fresh garlic
3 tbsp. olive oil
2 tbsp. parsley
pasta

1. Cut Salmon fillet in cubes. Let simmer in a pan with water and cook through.

2. Once cooked , flake the salmon. Boil salted water and add Pasta once ready. In a pan or Pot add the Olive oil, garlic and cook until lightly brown.

3. Add mushrooms and vodka to the pot and cook for 1 minute, stirring constantly. Add Tomato Sauce, Whipping Cream, Salmone, Parsley and Salt and pepper to taste.

4. Cook for 15mins. Once Pasta is ready add to the sauce and Serve.

Van Dyke Café
846 Lincoln Road, Miami Beach, FL

"Anybody who believes that the way to a man's heart is through his stomach flunked geography."
Robert Byrne

Yuca Fries with Cilantro Mayonnaise

Versailles Restaurant, The World's Most Famous Cuban Restaurant, has been serving tasty Cuban cuisine and culture to the South Florida community and tourists from around the world for four decades. Soon after it opened its doors in 1971, Versailles quickly became the gathering place and unofficial town square for Miami's Cuban exiles. Today, it remains the unrelenting gauge of the community's pulse.

2 lb. yucca, peeled
1 C. mayonnaise
2 tbsp. chopped fresh cilantro
2 tsp. lime juice
1 tsp. chopped garlic
¼ tsp. salt
⅛ tsp. cayenne pepper (optional)
vegetable oil (about 4 C.)

1. Cook yucca in boiling salted water in a Dutch oven 30 minutes or until fork-tender. Dry thoroughly with paper towels, and spread on baking sheets to cool. Cut each into ¼-inch-thick fries, and set aside.

2. Combine mayonnaise, next 4 ingredients, and, if desired, cayenne pepper in a small bowl.

3. Pour oil to depth of 3 inches into a Dutch oven, and heat to 350°. Fry yucca, in 3 or 4 batches, 6 minutes per batch. Drain on paper towels. Return oil to 350°, and fry yucca, in 3 or 4 batches, another 6 minutes or until crispy.

4. Drain on paper towels, and season with additional salt, if desired. Serve with cilantro mayonnaise.

3555 Southwest 8th Street, Miami, FL

Versailles

"I am the literary equivalent of a Big Mac and fries."
Stephen King

Wagons West Restaurant serves Breakfast all day as well as Daily Specials and Dinner Menus. Monday is Italian Night, Spaghetti and Meatballs, and Italian Food. Tuesday is BBQ Night. Wednesday is Blackened Night. Thursday is Country Night. Friday is Fish Night. Saturday Night Quesadillas, Marinated Chicken, or Steak. Local to Pinecrest 33156, Palmetto Bay, 33157, and neighboring communities.

1 egg
2 tsp. seafood seasoning (recommended: Old Bay Seasoning)
½ C. mayonnaise
¼ C. panko (Japanese breadcrumbs)
1 tsp. gingerroot juice or powder
1 tsp. hot sauce (recommended: Tabasco)
1 lemon, juiced
3 Tbsp. grapeseed oil
1 lb. lump crab, picked
all-purpose flour, for dusting

1. In a large bowl, thoroughly mix the egg, seafood seasoning, mayonnaise, breadcrumbs, ginger juice or powder, hot sauce, lemon juice, and oil. Add the crab and blend into the mixture, being careful not to break up the lumps of meat. Refrigerate for 30 minutes to 1 hour.

2. Portion the crab into 2-ounce cakes and lightly dust with flour. Heat a skillet over medium heat with the oil. Add the cakes and saute until golden brown, 2 to 3 minutes. Flip and cook on the second side until golden brown, 2 to 3 minutes. Repeat the process until all the cakes have been cooked.

Wagons West

11311 South Dixie Highway, Miami, FL

"If I was made of cake I'd eat myself before somebody else could."
Emma Donoghue, Room

Chilled Tomato-Lime Soup with Lobster Salad

A recipient of the Mobil Travel Guide Four-Star Award 2001-2009, The Hotel's romantic indoor/outdoor restaurant, Wish, also boasts a prestigious AAA Four Diamond rating. Wish's interior décor by fashion designer Todd Oldham is both exotic and cozy, while the exterior boasts a magical, tropical garden setting that is without a doubt, one of the most romantic al fresco dining areas in South Florida. The "Inner Garden" also evokes the lush outdoors with lush, tropical plants surrounding a delightfully intimate indoor dining area.

For Soup:
6 each Roma tomatoes, cored
⅛ C. lime juice
⅓ fluid ounce extra virgin olive oil
¼ tsp. cinnamon
⅛ pc. star anise
⅔ tbsp. sugar

For Salad:
1 lb. lobster meat, cooked, cut in 1" pcs.
⅞ each chayote squash, sliced ½" thick
⅛ bunch basil, julienned
⅛ lb. arugula, julienned
⅓ fluid oz. extra virgin oil
¼ each avocado, diced

For Soup:
1. With skin on, rub the tomatoes with the oil, salt and pepper. On a very hot grill, char the tomatoes on at least 75% of their surface. Remove and cool.
2. Rough chop the tomatoes into piece about 1" x 1" so they will be easily blended in a blender.
3. Blend all remaining ingredients in a blender, and strain through a fine sieve.
4. Season to taste. Chill for at least one hour.

For Salad:
1. Rub the chayote with oil, salt and pepper and mark them on the grill until tender. Remove, cool, dice and reserve.
2. Combine the lobster, chayote, avocado, basil and arugula withe olive oil, salt and pepper.

To Plate:
1. Divide the salad equally among 8 large soup bowls. Pour about 8 ounces of chilled soup into each bowl. Garnish with fresh basil and serve with a crisp white wine, for example a Pinot Gris.

801 Collins Avenue, Miami Beach, FL

Wish Restaurant

"My greatest strength is common sense. I'm really a standard brand - like Campbell's tomato soup or Baker's chocolate."
Katharine Hepburn

Bing Cherry Pie

Yardbird Southern Table & Bar is owned by 50 Eggs Restaurant Group, a development and management company operating multiple concepts from fine dining to fast-casual. Founded by John Kunkel, an industry veteran, 50 Eggs also owns and operates the Lime Fresh Mexican Grill brand, currently with 12 locations in the southeast, another 7 opening this year and expansion plans for an additional 200 throughout the East Coast by 2020.

4 C. Bing cherries, pitted
2 tbsp. fresh orange juice
2 tbsp. fresh lemon juice
2 tbsp. cornstarch
1 to 1½ C. sugar (depending on the sweetness of the fruit)
¼ tsp. ground cinnamon
Pinch of salt
¼ tsp. almond extract
1 tbsp. grated orange zest
1½ tbsp. cold unsalted butter, cut into small pcs.

1. Preheat the oven to 450°F. Prepare the Classic Pie Crust as directed for a 9-inch double-crust pie.

2. Place the cherries in a large bowl. Mix orange and lemon juices with the cornstarch, then combine with sugar, cinnamon, and salt. Toss with the cherries. Let rest for 15 minutes.

3. Add the almond extract and the orange zest; toss well.

4. Line a 9-inch pie plate with one crust and prick all over with a fork. Spoon the cherry filling evenly into the crust. Dot all over with butter. Cover with a top crust. With water, moisten the crusts where they meet, then turn the top crust under the bottom and flute the edge. Cut a few slits in the top to allow steam to escape. Decorate the surface if you wish by rolling out the scraps and cutting several cherry, leaf, and stem shapes.

5. Bake pie in center of the oven for 10 minutes at 450°F. Reduce heat to 350°F and bake 45 to 55 minutes more, or until the crust is nicely golden. Let cool on a rack before serving warm or at room temperature.

Yardbird Southern Table & Bar
1600 Lenox Avenue, Miami Beach, FL

"We must have a pie. Stress cannot exist in the presence of a pie."
David Mamet, Boston Marriage

Sesame Cold Noodle

Yeung's is quality Chinese food at very reasonable prices. Their take-out service is very, very speedy. They have good-sized lunch and dinner combinations that are less than $10 (and come with soup & fried rice, and an egg roll with dinner). The menu is huge - mainly because they have the traditional Chinese food options, but also a huge selection of "Cantonese" selections. The service was great! Very friendly family owned restaurant.

3 Tbsp. soy sauce
2 Tbsp. rice vinegar
½ tsp. hot pepper flakes
2 Tbsp. brown sugar
½ C. creamy peanut butter
1 Tbsp. toasted sesame oil
1 tsp. grated gingerroot
½ C. chicken broth
1 lb. linguine
chopped scallion
cucumber
sesame seed (to garnish)

1. In saucepan over medium heat, mix first 8 ingredients together (soy sauce to chicken broth), stir until thick and smooth.

2. Cook linguine in salted water until al dente. Drain and rinse with cool water.

3. Mix linguine and sauce mixture in bowl.

4. Serve cold or at room temperature with scallions, cucumbers, and sesame seeds as garnish.

Yeung's Chinese Restaurant
954 West 41st Street, Miami Beach, FL

Censure is a limp noodle across the wrist of the president.
I think the way we vote on the articles will express the
way we feel stronger than any censure vote.
Larry Craig

Lobster Miso Soup

The design was created by tokyo based noriyoshi muramatsu of studio glitt, formerly of the world renowned design house super potato. As with each ZUMA since the first one opened in london in 2002, muramatsu preserves the concept behind ZUMA's interior, while incorporating the natural products and textures present in each location.

2 lobster heads
3 tbsp. miso
3 tbsp. finely sliced scallions
⅓ oz. konbu/kelp. about 3 inches
6 C. water
3 tbsp. of wakame (dried seaweed)
½ C. katsuobushi (dried bonito flakes)
soy sauce, optional (i did not add to the soup)

1. Soak 3 inch of kelp in a saucepan with 6 cups of cold water for 30 min. Set the saucepan over medium heat. Just before the water comes to a boil (you will see bubbles and it takes about 10 min), remove kelp.

2. Bring to a boil and add 1 cup of bonito flakes. Simmers for a few min. Pour the soup through fine strainer, discard bonito shavings.

3. Return the dashi to the saucepan over low heat. Add the wakame and continue to simmer for a couple minutes until it open up and increase in size. Remove wakame using a fine strainer. Set aside.

4. Bring the dashi to boil. Add the miso paste and stir until dissolved.

5. Add the reserved lobsters to the dashi and cook for 10 minutes.

6. Stir in scallions and the reserved wakame. Serve immediately.

Zuma
270 Biscayne Boulevard Way, Miami, FL

"The preparation of good food is merely another expression of art, one of the joys of civilized living..."
Dione Lucas

Cheese Tortellini

In August 1986, Zuperpollo was born. The original name bore the S of superman, but to my surprise another business was using the name and so I decided to change the S for Z and dress the flying chicken like Zorro, which turned out less expensive than litigation. In its inception, we would open a franchise of chicken restaurants, but when I took to working in the kitchen and creating a menu, nostalgia for an Uruguayan restaurant as I had experienced with my own recipes and my own personal touch, and not being dependent on a chef allowed me to maintain consistency in the flavor of the foods.

2 Tbsp. olive oil
2 cloves garlic, cut in half
1 lb. bulk pork sausage
3 C. Prego® Roasted Garlic and Herb Italian Sauce
1 C. frozen peas
¾ C. heavy cream
16 oz. uncooked frozen cheese tortellini
1 pkg. (10 oz) Pepperidge Farm® Five Cheese Garlic Bread
½ C. grated Parmesan cheese

1. Heat the oven to 400 degrees F. for the bread.

2. Heat the oil in a 12-inch skillet over medium heat. Add the garlic and cook until it's golden brown. Remove the garlic from the skillet and set it aside. Add the sausage and cook until it's well browned, stirring often. Pour off any fat.

3. Stir the sauce in the skillet and heat to a boil. Stir the garlic, peas and cream in the skillet. Reduce the heat to low. Cook and stir for 5 minutes or until the mixture is hot and bubbling.

4. Cook the tortellini according to the package directions. Drain the tortellini well in a colander. Meanwhile, bake the bread according to the package directions.

5. Stir the tortellini in the skillet. Sprinkle with the cheese. Cut the bread into 2-inch diagonal slices. Serve the bread with the tortellini.

Zuperpollo
1247 Coral Way, Miami, FL

"It's so beautifully arranged on the plate - you know someone's fingers have been all over it."
Julia Child

Signature Tastes of MIAMI

Steven W. Siler is a firefighter-cum-chef serving in Bellingham, Washington. Long marinated in the epicurean heritage of the Deep South, Steven has spent over 20 years (dear God has it been that long?!) in the much-vaulted restaurant industry from BOH to FOH to chef. In addition, he has served as an editor and contributing writer for several food publications. When not trying to shove food down his fellow firefighters' gullets, he enjoys sailing and sampling the finest of scotches and

wines, and has an irrational love affair with opera. He swears one day he will relive the above picture on the Gulf Coast with a good Will.

The Signature Tastes series of cookbooks is the one of the first of a series of culinary celebrations from Smoke Alarm Media, based in the Pacific Northwest. Smoke Alarm Media is named for another series of unfortunate culinary accidents at an unnamed fire department, also in the Pacific Northwest. One of the founders was an active firefighter. Having been trained as a chef, he found himself in the position of cooking frequently at the fire station. Alas, his culinary skills were somewhat lacking in using the broiler and smoke would soon fill the kitchen and station. The incidents became so frequent that the 911 dispatch would call the station and ask if "Chef Smoke Alarm" would kindly refrain from cooking on his shift. Thus Smoke Alarm Media was born.

| SIGNATURE TASTES | HIDDEN EATS | TABLE FACTS | BYGONE ERAS | ART OF CULINARY DIPLOMACY | VARSITY |

CPSIA information can be obtained at www.ICGtesting.com
Printed in the USA
BVOW09s1140050615

403415BV00003B/4/P